Understanding the *Blessing*

Apostle Gregory Mitchell

© Copyright 2016 by Apostle Gregory Mitchell. All rights reserved under national and international copyright laws. Expressed written permission must be secured from the author and publisher, Apostle Gregory Mitchell to use or reproduce any part of this book, except for brief quotations in critical reviews or articles.

Unless otherwise noted, Scripture quotations are taken from the KING JAMES VERSION (*KJV*) of the Holy Bible. Amplified quotations are indicated as (*AMP*). New Living Translation quotations are indicated as (*NLT*). All versions used by permission of the copyright owners according to required citations and references.

Published in North Carolina by:

Gregory Mitchell

North Carolina

In conjunction with Carsamonte Publishing

Editorial services:

First-line and developmental editing: Carmen Glover, Carsamonte, CarsamontePublishing@gmail.com

Proofing: Carmen Glover

Cover Design by: Quik Graphicz Creative Co., Hope Mills, North Carolina

Interior Design by: Carmen TheWordsmith

Understanding the Blessing was printed in the United States of America.

Copyright © 2015 Apostle Gregory Mitchell

All rights reserved.

ISBN-13: 978-0-9830614-8-9

DEDICATION

This book is dedicated to my beloved wife, Carla, who has shared and provided me with thirty-five years of unwavering love. I thank you for the inspiration and support you exemplified as you inspired me to become all that God created me to be *(whether through writing or preaching)*. You made all the difference in my life as my friend, lover, and wife. It is my prayer that God continues to bless and cause his unmerited favor to rest, rule, and forever abide upon your life. You *are* the love of my life!

To my sons, Gregory Seantāe and Reginald Ian; in you I am well pleased. It is my desire that you accomplish all God has placed in your hands. Thank you for your prayers for my success, as well as your labor in ministry. Continue to be strengthened in the Lord and the power of His might! To Princess, my daughter; I love you beyond words and appreciate every effort and prayer. Thank you for your loyal service in various capacities and all you do to make my life and ministry a success. Your help is truly appreciated. Continue to accomplish all God has for you, and may His blessings rest upon you.

To my sisters, Hattie Baker, Laney S. McIntosh, and Sally Mitchell, I so love and appreciate all of you. Thank you for your love, support, and gifts of love. Thank you for standing by me when times were both good and bad. It is through your encouragement that I am able to stand and continue in the things of the Lord. A very special thanks to my mother-in-law, Ms. Geneva McIntosh who has stood by my side supporting me day-after-day. Thank you for your love and support. Most of all, thank you for being a true intercessor for me. Your prayers and words of love have encouraged me the most.

Finally, I want to acknowledge the members of *Breath of Life International Ministries*. Thank you for the love and support you exemplify, not only to me, but to my family. Your support has been overwhelming. I speak the blessings of the Lord upon you all! *Thank you!*

CONTENTS

	Acknowledgments	ii
1	Where it all Began	1
2	Satan Tricks Adam	16
3	The Results of the Curse	31
4	Abraham; the Chosen Vessel	43
5	The Blessing Upon Isaac	66
6	Jacob Receives the Blessing	73
7	The Blessing Upon Joseph	87
8	The Blessing Upon Hannah	105
9	Hidden Revelations	112
10	The Blessing Upon Jesus	121
11	The Blessing Upon the Body of Christ	135
	Conclusion	144
	About the Author	146

ACKNOWLEDGMENTS

This book is for everyone who desires change. *Understanding the Blessing* will revolutionize your entire life by offering you a life of prosperity and success. If this book is received, it will inspire you to assess the anointing in your life. The blessing is our true connection to the prosperous life. For this reason, God sent his Son, Jesus that we might obtain the God abundant life.

"The thief comes only in order to steal and kill and destroy. I came that they may have and enjoy life, and have it in abundance (to the full, till it overflows)."

(John 10:10, *AMP*)

Gregory Mitchell

CHAPTER 1
Where it all Began

My aim is to reveal where the blessing originated and how it affected man and animal. For many years, the church (*body of Christ*) failed to recognize the intent and the purpose for the blessing. My objective is to impart a greater revelation of the blessing and cause you to prosper in every area of your life. For this to happen, we must locate its origin and determine how the blessing empowers man. Without locating the source, properly interpreting how the blessing operates will virtually be impossible. Let's begin with our foundational Scripture:

"The blessing of the Lord- it makes [truly] rich, and He adds no sorrow with it [neither does toiling increase it]." (Proverbs 10:22, *AMP*)

In my early years of ministry, I constantly heard about the blessing of the Lord. In most churches, you could not enter without someone saying, *"I'm blessed and highly favored."* I heard this phrase so much until I wanted to define its meaning.

As I inquired, I found that most Christians spoke of things they didn't comprehend. Immediately, my curiosity heightened and I desired to learn more.

With great hunger, I began to search the Bible. As I examined and meditated on certain Scriptures, the Lord impressed upon me to write this book. As you read, God will broaden the capability of your mind, empowering you with revelation. This is how we'll begin. Where it all started.

We'll examine Proverbs 10:22, which provides insight concerning the blessing. This Scripture emphasizes that the blessing of the Lord makes us rich. To gain insight of this Scripture, we must identify where the blessing began and how it originated. The blessing is a topic that has been misunderstood for generations. In this hour of refreshing, God is releasing revelation that will transform the minds of believers.

As we observe Genesis 1:1, it declares, *"In the beginning God created the heaven and the earth."* This Scripture denotes the oneness of the divine Trinity. It establishes God as the creator and not the theory of evolution. The Bible provides evidence as to God creating both Heaven and Earth from the beginning, before there was man and before there was evolution; be it in theory or in the literal sense.

The following verse indicates God arranging and establishing the entire universe. Throughout time, scientists have tried to explain the formation of the universe. We certainly thank them for their studies. However, the Bible explains how the universe was created and fashioned by the Word of God. This is our true conviction of faith.

"Through faith we understand that the worlds were framed by the word of God, so that things which are seen were not made of things which do appear." (Hebrews 11:3) Fred Gottlieb stated, *"Once again, we find in Psalm 104 the idea of God as the constant Sustainer as well as the Creator."*[1]

Several times the Scriptures mention, *"God said."* This denotes his magnificent power as He spoke the universe into existence. Here, God is recognized as the creator and sustainer of the universe through *words*. The Holy Scriptures emphasizes that God blesses (creates or empowers) with his Word.

"And God created great whales, and every living creature that moveth, which the waters brought forth abundantly, after their kind, and every winged fowl after his kind: and God saw that it was good. And God blessed them, saying, Be fruitful, and multiply, and fill the waters in the seas, and let fowl multiply in the earth."

(Genesis 1:21-22)

This passage provides insight as to how God blesses or empowers. My primary objective is mankind. I will not scrutinize this Scripture but will provide revelation at a later time. We cannot understand the blessing without examining how

---

[1] Fred Gottlieb, "The Creation Theme in Genesis 1, Psalm 104 and Job 38-42," *Jewish Bible Quarterly (Online)* 44, no. 1 (January 2016): 32.

it affected the animals.

The blessing was executed from the time God spoke in Genesis chapter one. The blessing which empowered the universe is the same anointing that empowered the animals and man. This is one of the missing elements to understanding where the blessing originated. Without pin-pointing the origin, the blessing will not be properly understood.

Many of you might question how this can be. Simple! Nothing can exist or have life without God. He is the author and creator of life and without Him, there is no life. For life to exist, it must originate from the life-giver; God. For this reason, God said, *"Let there be light."*

God is the one who *"Empowers"* all aspects of life and He does so through His Word. In verse twenty-two, the blessing was spoken over the animals. Notice what God said, *"Be fruitful and multiply."* His word released the anointing to work in the lives of the animals. Without the anointing, they could not multiply. The power lied within the anointing. What a powerful word spoken by God! What words are you speaking day after day? *"Death and life are in the power of the tongue."* (Proverbs 18:21)

As we examine verse twenty-six, it is in the mind of God to create man (mankind). Man, was to be like God; possessing the ability to speak like God. God created man and man was to be like Him; a type of creator. In Genesis 1:26, Believers are empowered with the legal right to walk and live with this type of authority. What authority do you possess in your life? Regardless of the type, it originated from God.

In Genesis 1:28, God gave dominion and authority to man. They were to rule over the Earth. Understanding this could resolve many of today's marital problems recognizing that man *"which includes that of woman,"* had authority to rule and reign. In today's society, women are told that they aren't rulers like men. This, a lack of interpretation concerning authority, destroys marriages.

In the perfect will of God, man and woman were to rule over the works of God's hand. This included the *"resources"* made available to them. Somehow, we failed to recognize that this also included money. In the covenant relationship of marriage, many times the wife manages finances more prudently than her husband. My aim is to enlighten the body of Christ of the excellence of *"oneness"* and not to discourage anyone.

Husbands, your wives may be a better planners or managers in finances. If so, allow her to use the precious gift God has bestowed upon her. This will create an atmosphere for your finances to excel. As this is implemented, stress and financial struggles will cease. If we are to be men of integrity, being free from financial stress, worries, and anxieties is what we really want. Please stop and mediate on this!

Jesus died and committed the works of the Father into the hands of Believers. All we have to do is to accept what He did. Isaiah 45:11 emphasizes how Christians command the hand of God and provides clarity as to the authority Jesus gave. *"Thus saith the Lord, the Holy One of Israel, and his Maker, Ask me of things to come concerning my sons, and concerning the work of my hands command ye me."*

As Christians, it is our responsibility to walk in the authority and power given by Jesus. We have the power to command things and speak them into existence. There is nothing we cannot accomplish through the Word of God. As Jesus walked the Earth and commanded things, so can we. I will not expound on the authority and power we possess, however, it is important to realize that this power and authority is available to everyone who puts their faith in Christ Jesus.

God empowers man

How does this relate to life? If we think about life without prosperity, it would be meaning-less. For a better understanding, think about Adam and Eve on the Earth without any creatures of their kind. It would have been impossible for them to talk or relate to other humans or do any of the things we do today with our spouses and friends. Why? Because without the empowerment, only Adam and Eve would have existed. Now, do you understand the importance of prosperity? What would your life be like without prosperity? Please stop and meditate on this.

The word *prosperity* derives from the root-word *prosper*. Prosperity is not the problem. The problem lies in our understanding. Many Christians have an understanding of prosperity as only *"money."* True prosperity is, *"being in control of any and every situation that comes your way."* This means you are self-sufficient and well able to provide for yourself and others. *"And God is able to make all grace (every favor and earthly blessing) come to you in abundance, so that you may always and under all circumstances and whatever the need be self-sufficient [possessing enough to require no aid or support and furnished in abundance for every good work and charitable donation]."* (2 Corinthians 9:8. *AMP*)

God knew that man would need many things to live the life He intended. For this reason, God empowered man to prosper; creating an avenue for his needs to be met. Truly, the will of the Lord is for man to prosper. If any doubt has hindered you concerning prosperity, this book will help you to appreciate God's will for your life.

As we explore how God empowers man, it is interesting to know God empowers in the same manner as men empowers one another. This pertains to life in ways we have never understood. In today's society, after electing candidates into office, they must be inaugurated. The word inaugurate is defined as, *"To empower or to endow"* with power.

During the ceremony, words are spoken over the individual's life empowering him or her to execute their office. The power lies in the words spoken over the individual. Where does the power lie? In the words! It makes no difference whether God's Word or man's words. The results are the same;

empowerment takes place.

Genesis 1:26 denotes this is where it began. God blessed both man and woman by empowering them with the anointing. The word *blessed* must be defined in biblical terminology. In verse twenty-eight, it is defined in the Hebrew language as, *"Barak"* which means, *"to invoke a benediction."* The word *"benediction"* in the Roget's 21st Century Thesaurus means, *"blessing, consecration, laying on of hands."* Consecration is another word for the anointing.

John 20:22 provides insight as to the invoking of a benediction: *"to speak or pronounce a blessing upon."* Jesus invoked a blessing upon His disciples as He breathed upon them. His breath was the Holy Spirit. Isaiah 55:11 exemplifies the power of the Word of God. When Jesus spoke, it was done.

God's word never returns to Him void when He is the only one involved. Often, it is said, *"If God said it; He will bring it to pass."* I received revelation of this phrase and this is not always true. Believe it or not, most prophets or great men of God have spoken the word of the Lord. However, when God's word is between God and man, sometimes an individual fails to add corresponding actions. To that end, there is no manifestation. The lack of manifestation was not God. The word was between God and man. The individual had a work to do. If he or she fails to apply corresponding actions, the result will always be no manifestation. According to Dr. Creflo Dollar, *"The corresponding actions are born out of an individual's faith in*

God."[2]

As we reflect on John 20:22, Jesus executes the same act God performed in Genesis 1:28. The apostles received the blessing. Jesus empowered them with the anointing. This is where I will define the blessing. I credit Dr. Dollar as he says, *"It is God's supernatural ability empowering you for success."*[3] It is an empowerment that transforms every area of your life.

Some of you may question within yourselves and say, *"I thought they received the Holy Spirit on the day of Pentecost."* There are times when we read, we fail to get an understanding of what we have read. Surely, this has happened to us all. Therefore, possessing knowledge of what we read is essential. This empowerment can manifest as God's favor. It makes no difference how you define the blessing; it all works together.

To understand what happened on the Day of Pentecost, we must identify *Pentecost*. It is known as the fiftieth day from Passover. Boisclair depicts Pentecost as, *"While the Gospel of John reports that Jesus conferred the Holy Spirit upon his disciples when he first appeared to them in the evening of his resurrection* (John 20:22), Acts reports that this occurred fifty days later."[4] Acts 2:1-4 provides insight about the empowerment of man through the Holy Spirit. Verse one refers to a period

---

[2] Creflo A. Dollar, "How Faith and Grace Works Together," *Lecture, Grace Institute*, World Changers Church International, College Park, Ga, June 15-17, 2016.

[3] Ibid.

[4] Regina A. Boisclair, et al. "Pentecost Vigil, and Pentecost Day," *Homily Service* 43, no. 2 (February 2010): 166.

which represents a beginning point. As the day approached, it was declared as the *Day of Pentecost*. This represented the fulfilling of the fiftieth day.

As the day climaxed, the Holy Spirit descended into the hearts of the apostles empowering them with the anointing. This is known as the *indwelling* of the Spirit. In other words, they were baptized with the Holy Spirit. Jesus breathed on them but the demonstration of power was exemplified on the *Day of Pentecost*.

As we further our examination of John 20:22, the word *"breathed"* is mentioned. It is also mentioned in Genesis 2:7. The correlation between the usages of this word has considerable insight regarding the empowerment of man. The word *"breathed"* is derived from the word breath. Webster's Dictionary defines breathed as, *"to say or utter."* The word usage for both Scriptures mean, *"to speak."* This indicates that God spoke man into existence.

God's Intended Purpose

Genesis 1:28 is insight into the blessing. God anointed Adam and Eve empowering them with the ability to be fruitful and multiply. The word fruitful is defined as, *"to be productive."* Webster's Dictionary defines productive as, *"having the power to produce plentifully."* Therefore, the purpose for the anointing is to empower you to live the God abundant life.

The blessing, when understood and properly administrated, empowers every area of your life. Greatness lies within the anointing. As we understand the intended purpose, the importance of the anointing is revealed. The blessing makes us more like God. God desires that His children prosper. He empowers us to be as He is: *prosperous*.

In Genesis 1:28, the word *"multiply"* is mentioned. Webster's Dictionary defines the word multiply as, *"to make or become more numerous."* The meaning of this word denotes increase. The blessing causes increase to come into your life. Without the anointing, the life of a Believer would be limited. This limitation applies to both the physical and spiritual realm. The blessing removes all the limitations.

The Existence of the Dinosaurs

In this section, my aim is to inspire you to research material Paleontologists have proclaimed for years. They believe Dinosaurs lived and colonized the earth during a specific time. Upon careful examination of several Scriptures, this era Paleontologists proclaimed as, *"The Dinosaurs Age"*[5] may have existed. I will not validate their studies or condemn their discoveries. My primary objective is the truth.

It is evident that God created the heavens and the earth. Before God recreated the Earth, it was already in existence. My evidence proves the earth's existence before man. Acknowledging Paleontologists for their work, God revealed certain revelations to them. *"In the beginning God created the*

---

[5] www.kidcyber.com.au/topics/dinosaurs.htm.

heaven and the earth. And the earth was without form, and void; and darkness was upon the face of the deep. And the Spirit of God moved upon the face of the waters." (Genesis 1:1-2)

During this time, the earth was filled with darkness. This may be the period in which Paleontologists believed Dinosaurs existed. I am not a scientist, but as we examine the Scriptures, things begin to add up. The word *"darkness"* is mentioned in the above Scripture; however, physical darkness is not necessarily the case. It always amazes me how most people perceive the natural things first; *"the absence of God is darkness."* God's presence was absent from the earth.

As the reader, I want you to visualize seeing these huge animals eating and destroying the Earth. Many of you have had the opportunity to watch such movies as *Jurassic Park* and others, which exemplifies the nature of these colossal beasts. For years, they destroyed the Earth (the region God placed them) leaving it lifeless. Adam's sin did not only affect the life of mankind, but the animals. The curse of sin caused dinosaurs to destroy one another.

As we examine the above Scripture, it emphasizes the importance of *why* God anointed man. It is important to know that the Earth (the area dinosaurs existed) was destroyed because of these animals. Can you imagine how empty and void of life the Earth was? They completely demolished the life earth produced. If the earth was to survive, God would have to recreate life once again.

The dinosaurs destroyed the region where God positioned them; so, God commanded Adam and Eve to replenish the Earth. In other words, Adam and Eve were to cover the Earth with the glory of God. They were to multiply and expand across the entire globe. I have learned over time that Creationist believe dinosaurs lived during the time of Adam's existence, but were placed within a region apart from man. This makes sense, because there was no death until Adam sinned. Consequently, dinosaurs could not have existed and died before the sin of man. Adam's sin gave birth to death by which all creatures including man must die. This is an on-going debate between scholars and theologians. Their argument stems from Genesis 1:1-2. There are several theories concerning this time frame, but it depends on which theory you believe.

Adam's Responsibility to the Garden

It is obvious that the purpose of the blessing is more than fruitfulness and multiplication. One of its purposes is to empower you to work. Often, I use the word *"work"* and refer to it as an, *"offal"* word. Why? I have discovered that most people hate the word *"work."* This is not an offal word but sometimes viewed in this manner. God has empowered you to work. Adam had a responsibility to work the garden.

Another intended purpose for the blessing is to remove lack. What is lack? Webster's Dictionary defines lack as, *"the fact or state of being absent or needed."* Most people define lack as what a person does not possess materially. Lack is far greater than what a person fails to possess materially, but intellectually.

As we explore Adam's responsibility, Psalm 115:16 denotes God's purpose for the earth. *"The heaven, even the heavens, are the Lord's: but the earth hath he given to the children of men."* The significance of this Scripture provides clarity on God releasing the earth to man. For this reason, God placed Adam in the garden to dress and keep it. The word *dress* is defined as, *"to keep in, to tend and guard,"* while the word *keep* means, *"to protect or preserve."* Adam's responsibility was to protect the Garden of Eden. God gave the Earth to man and in return, it was to become likened to the Garden of Eden.

In the New Testament, Jesus restored the blessing. As Christians, we must use the power and authority given to us. This awesome power is obtainable and is available to all who accepts Christ. The time has come for Believers to rise up and possess the things God has for them.

As God charged Adam to manage the garden, He explained to him concerning an intruder. *"An intruder is one who thrusts himself, or enters illegal."* I refuse to believe that God failed to warn Adam concerning the intruder. I believe God informed Adam and instructed him to be constantly aware of the enemy. As a matter of fact, the word God spoke to Adam clarifies that God fully informed him.

Lucifer, also known as Satan, has been described as *the angel that committed an act of sin which led to his dethroning.* He was the anointed Cherubim; full of beauty and second in command. Somehow, we have assumed that God found sin in Lucifer which led to his dethrone. Before being dethroned, Lucifer was known for walking up and down in the Earth. Our interpretation of Lucifer's fall may be diminished by false perception. Although Jesus said, *"And He said to them, I saw Satan falling like a lightning [flash] from heaven."* (Luke 10:18, *AMP*) Is this what Jesus meant?

According to Job 2, Satan found himself walking up and down the Earth; a place he would often spend time. After receiving a greater understanding of what occurred in the garden, I can now say that man created Satan, not God. God created Lucifer. Although Lucifer was the anointed Cherubim, God had anointed Adam to be like Him. Adam's anointing consisted of unconditional authority. Therefore, Lucifer, as found in Isaiah 14 desired to possess this anointing which would make him like God.

After realizing the power and authority Adam possessed, Lucifer began to fashion his deceptive plan to deceive the heart of man. For this reason, we must always guard and protect the anointing. This is one of the reasons Satan exists. He is after the precious anointing. Satan strives to find the precious soul who fails to protect his or her self with the armor of God.

Satan is always on the move and never gives up. He delights in his assignment day and night. We must always be alert and aware of his strategies. The Apostle Paul warned Believers not to be ignorant of his devices. I would advise you to guard the anointing on your life. The blessing is so precious that Satan will kill for it. Yes, he will kill for it! You cannot afford to let your guard down at any time. You must remain focused and in control.

With the beginning of a new century, God is revealing truths; some you have heard and some you have not. It is God who gives the increase, and increase you will receive. My prayer is that you will inquire about God, and not the things of this world. The blessing is enough to get excited about.

As we learn about Satan, it will be interesting to observe how this angelic being operates. Most people fail to realize that Satan is very manipulative. This is one of his favorite techniques. As we continue, the mindset of Satan will be revealed. To further our awareness, let's explore his plans to determine how Satan will deceive Adam in hopes of gaining the blessing on Adam's life.

CHAPTER 2
Satan Tricks Adam

My aim in this chapter is to expose the plan of Satan. I want to reveal how he through deception deceived Adam and Eve. Until we recognize the mindset of Satan, he will have the upper hand. Any area of life where knowledge is absent, Satan can and will defeat you. For this reason, we must educate ourselves and obtain knowledge in every area of life, *"Lest Satan should get an advantage of us: for we are not ignorant of his devices."* (2 Corinthians 2:11)

The word *"devices"* is mentioned in the King James Version. According to Webster's Dictionary, it is defined as, *"to trick."* It is also mentioned in Ephesians 6:11, though the word in this passage is *"wiles,"* the meaning is the same as devices. We must be alert to resist the trickery of the devil.

The Bible states that God created Adam and Eve. Many

times, *"Eve"* is referred to as the woman. I call her, *"The first woman Adam."* Some of you may ask why. The woman was named Eve after they sinned. Sin changed them and it is changing people today. After their sin, she received the name Eve.

When they disobeyed God, they were saying within themselves; we will no longer receive knowledge from God, but from the world. Some Saints today are not looking to God for knowledge and understanding. They are finding themselves looking to the world's system for answers. The answers you need *are* in God. When we decide to seek after the world's way of doing things, we limit ourselves. This type of mindset will always cause you to live outside the *"True Oneness"* of God.

Adam and Eve lived in harmony for many years. They were of one heart, soul, and body. They needed only one name; *"Adam."* Sin divided the union causing them to think according to the flesh rather than the Spirit. Their thinking was in opposition to the Word of God. They were led totally by their emotions. We should never allow our emotions to dictate to us, especially, when our thoughts are not the thoughts of God. These thoughts will only lead to destruction.

God's plans are for man's good. Satan's plans are for man's destruction. God's plans for your life include the blessing. Once again, the purpose for the blessing is to empower you for success. The anointing is for your good. One of its main purposes is to destroy every yoke in your life. The anointing on

Jesus caused many individuals that were lame, blind, afflicted, and diseased to be made whole. This same anointing does work today in the life of Believers.

> *How God anointed Jesus of Nazareth with the Holy Ghost and with power: who went about doing good, and healing all that were oppressed of the devil; for God was with him.* (Acts 10:38)

The blessing empowers every area of your life. One of Satan's plans is to block the anointing. His plans always include destruction. His ultimate goal is to destroy man. It was in Satan's plans to deceive Adam and gain the blessing. The question was how would this evil being deceive him? What tactics did he use to mislead Adam, and what tactics is he using today to deceive Believers? Let's further our study and explore the mindset of this evil creature and expose him for who he is.

The mindset of Satan

As the mindset of Satan is examined, I would like to reveal his intentions and how he used deception to deceive Adam. His motives and intentions became corrupt as he desired the anointing upon Adam's life. This was the beginning of his dethroning.

> *How art thou fallen from heaven, O Lucifer, son of the morning! how art thou cut down to the ground, which didst weaken the nations! For thou hast said in thine heart, I will ascend into heaven, I will exalt my throne above the stars of God: I will sit also upon the*

mount of the congregation, in the sides of the north: I will ascend above the heights of the clouds; I will be like the most High. (Isaiah 14:12-14)

According to this passage, the motives of Satan were never pure. He was the chief musician in Heaven. His assignment was to come before God every morning with praise and worship. Oh, how beautiful the praise and worship must have been! It is here where the mindset of Satan will be revealed.

In heaven, Lucifer was known as the anointed Cherubim. He possessed everything angels could only desire. This alone should tell us something! He possessed a beauty some of the angels desired. Day after day, some of the angels would say within them, *"I wish I was as beautiful as Lucifer."* His beauty and influence caused some of the angels to think different.

Recently, I discovered a remarkable revelation. Angels are not flawless as we were led to believe. All my life I thought angels were perfect. This may surprise some of you, God is the only perfect (without fault) spiritual being, and Jesus is next. All angels were created by God; however, they like you and I possess the power of choice.

The power of choice was given to man. God decided from the beginning of man's existence to provide man with the power of choice. It is in this component (soul's realm) that man as well as angels must learn obedience. It is here where I will interject this hidden revelation. How many times have you heard someone say, *"Jesus was the only perfect man to walk the earth?"* Even though this sounds good, it is not totally true.

To understand this, you must remain patient and open minded to receive the truth. Once, I asked my congregation; if a man were to be perfect, in what area would he have to obtain perfection? No one could answer the question. Do you know why? Most Christians believe that they cannot obtain perfection. What is perfection? *"The highest degree of proficiency, skill, or excellence, as in some art."*[6] All our lives, we have heard that Jesus was the only perfect man. This way of thinking has led many Christians to believe that they cannot achieve perfection. This has caused us to say within ourselves, *"this is an impossible task."*

After meditating on the life of Jesus, I immediately began to explain to my congregation that if a man is to be perfect, perfection would lie in his decisions. What do you mean in his decisions? This is the area of life where a man can fail or become successful. It's all about making right decisions. Life is a series of decisions. Perfection lies in your decisions. Jesus, though He was born spiritually innocent, faced sinful challenges daily but was perfect (reached full maturity) in his decisions.

> *So Jesus answered them by saying, I assure you, most solemnly I tell you, the Son is able to do nothing of Himself (of His own accord); but He is able to do only what He sees the Father doing, for whatever the Father*

---
[6] Online Dictionary: www.dictionary.com.

does is what the Son does in the same way [in His turn]. (John 5:19, *AMP*)

The above Scripture elucidates that Jesus did nothing outside the Father's will. No matter what the situation was, His decisions were not His own. This is what Adam should have done, as we must do. We must bring our decisions in line with God's will for our lives. How will this be done? By meditating in the Word of God and receiving the mind of Christ. This will cause us to become even as Jesus was; mature in our decisions.

Adam, though he failed, was perfect in his decisions until he was deceived. God permitted Adam to take responsibility for his actions. He did not blame him for his disobedience, but provided an opportunity for repentance. The Bible shows that Adam was deceived into disobedience. However, Christians today must not allow their decisions to be made through deception. Adam failed and we too will fail if our decisions are not in agreement with the Word of God.

In all your ways know, recognize, and acknowledge Him, and He will direct and make straight and plain your paths. (Proverbs 3:6, *AMP*)

Lucifer, as beautiful as he was, possessed all types of musical instruments. Musicians, his desire is for you to remain under his control. He wants you to dedicate your time, energy, and talents to him. Satan desires the glory for himself. He does not want you to praise God with your gifts and talents. His desire is for you to abandon God as he did. If Satan can get you to praise him, then he thinks that God will abandon you. Ha, ha, ha. Wrong!

God will *never* abandon you. His love is unconditional. You cannot earn or buy His love. God loves you whether you love Him or not. God's arms are open to receive and care for you. It is God who blessed you and He will love you whether you use your gifts for His glory or for the world. *"For God is love."* (1 John 4:8)

I am a musician and I thank God for blessing me with this precious gift. The heart of the Lord is that all musicians will submit their gifts and talents to Him. In return, multiplication occurs. Your gifts and talents were given to you for the Kingdom of God. I encourage you to submit your gifts and watch God develop a more excellent way.

In Ezekiel 28:13-19, the Prophet Ezekiel spoke the mind of God concerning Satan. I will not list this passage, but desire that you will read it in your spare time. According to this passage, Lucifer was God's anointed Cherubim. When God discovered iniquity in him, immediately, he was dethroned.

Verse fifteen indicates that he was created to obey God. However, as he focused on his beauty, self-adoration developed. In other words, his thinking changed. He no longer walked in obedience to God, but desired to obtain the honor and praise for himself. In his heart, these thoughts occurred; *"Hum, I can receive the praise that I offer God for myself."* This proves that his heart was corrupted and his motives were based in selfishness. Selfishness was found in Lucifer.

My prayer is for the readers of this book to possess a greater understanding of Satan. It doesn't matter how you slice or dice it; his mind is evil. The Bible refers to him as the evil genius; we should do the same. Satan never does anything good for anyone. He is always about self. Selfishness is one of his greatest weapons. Please do not allow yourself to become a victim of selfishness.

The mind of Satan has been revealed and his deceptive ways uncovered. At this point, Satan's desire is to possess the blessing. Let's determine the steps which lie in the plans of Satan. If he was clever enough to deceive Adam, he will certainly try to deceive you. Without God, we have no chance of defeating him. It is in our best interest to read the Bible and learn about both; God and Satan.

Satan Deceives Adam and the woman

Now I will reveal how Satan deceived Eve and how she persuaded Adam. Christians fail to understand what transpired in the garden. Because of their failure, my desire is to enlighten the Body of Christ with understanding that gives peace of mind.

Now the serpent was more subtle than any beast of the field which the LORD God had made. And he said unto the woman, Yea, hath God said, Ye shall not eat of every tree of the garden? (Genesis 3:1)

To obtain a greater interpretation of the above Scripture, the word "subtle" must be defined. According to Webster's

Dictionary it is defined as, *"cunning, prudent, crafty; always used in a bad sense."* This Scripture indicates that Satan embodied himself within the serpent. Why the serpent? They both possessed the same characteristics. The serpent was as cunning as Satan. Satan used a creature likened to himself.

Day after day, Satan seeks after the precious life. The precious life stems from the anointing. Why? The anointing makes the difference. The comparison can be as the difference between life and death. Death can be seen as the result of the one who fails to possess the anointing. It is referred to as *"the absence of God."* When we possess the blessing, the life of God stems from it.

It is obvious that Satan attempts to do whatsoever it takes to possess the anointing. In Genesis 3:1, he tempted the woman in hopes of a response from his acquisition. It was through this test that the woman responded. She fell into his bag of tricks. As time passed, she communed with Satan who is using the serpent to his advantage. Apparently, she failed to realize that no animal or beast had authority to speak. The serpent was out or order. God created man in his image and his likeness. Man, was the only speaking spirit outside of God.

I perceive that some of you are wondering what's going on! God had not permitted animals or beast to speak. Only Adam and Eve had legal authorization to speak. The serpent's ability to speak was prohibited. Through the disobedience of Adam, sin entered the world. Therefore, as God's punishment was implemented, both Satan and the serpent were punished.

In the plans of Satan, his desire was to get the woman to submit to him; and in return, Adam would submit to her. This is where I will reveal revelation knowledge. Satan knew the woman possessed the power [the ability] to persuade the man. He knew from the beginning that if he could persuade the woman, then Adam out of his love for his wife would submit to her. This is exactly what happened. In life today, men are constantly persuaded by women to do things that they know are not right.

In Genesis 3:6, Adam's presence appears to be unknown. The Scripture says, *"and gave also unto her husband with her; and he did eat."* It is important to determine his exact location. After carefully examining this Scripture, Adam is *within* the presence of his wife. He is not on the beach or at the lake; he is *with* his wife. How many times have you heard that Adam was off in la-la land? This is another reason to study for yourself. Adam failed to restrain his wife.

In the New Testament, Jesus came speaking the Word of God. Some of the Pharisees and scribes who heard Jesus speak would immediately return and examine the Holy Scriptures. Though they were religious people, they would not take someone's word without examining it. How can we do any less?

Today, some Christians fail to read and study for themselves. They constantly wait for the preacher to tell them everything about the Bible. This is not good nor is it safe. Never allow yourself to receive the word of an individual without knowing his or her background. It's your responsibility to study for yourself. For this reason, the Bible says, *"And we beseech you, brethren, to know them which labour among you, and are over you in the Lord, and admonish you."* (1 Thessalonians 5:12)

God gave a command to Adam in Genesis 2:16-17 which pertained to life or death. It was Adam's responsibility to inform his wife concerning this law. In today's society, God speaks to either the husband, or wife. It doesn't matter who He speaks to, the problem lies in our communication. Now, the question remains, did Adam communicate this law with his wife? Yes! The words she spoke in Genesis 3:2, 3 indicate that she knew what God commanded Adam. This is the proof of Adam's communication with his wife.

The Bible indicates that they failed to keep the Word of the Lord. It makes no difference how we try to examine their failure; they failed to obey. The tactics Satan used must be revealed in order for you to become knowledgeable of his devices. One of the devices Satan used was deception. According to Webster's Dictionary "deception" is defined as:

1. *The act of deceiving or misleading.*
2. *The state of being deceived or misled.*

According to these definitions, they were deceived by *"misleading information."* Satan, who is the father of lies, misled them through deception. How many times have you been deceived through misleading information? If you have been deceived, then you should understand how they failed.

It is obvious that Satan deceived them through deceptive information. What information did he use? Before I answer the question, several times I stated that they were deceived. It was not Adam deceived, but the woman. Adam submitted to the desires of his wife. He was not the one deceived by Satan's deception. The following Scripture emphasizes how Satan deceived Eve and what enticing words were used.

> *And the serpent said unto the woman, Ye shall not surely die: For God doth know that in the day ye eat thereof, then your eyes shall be opened, and ye shall be as gods, knowing good and evil.* (Genesis 3:4-5)

This Scripture indicates that Satan spoke to the woman. It was through the serpent that his words were heard. Notice the words that he spoke. They were so forceful that they caused her to ponder. As she pondered on the words, *"ye shall not surely die,"* he began to manipulate them by accusing God of withholding things. Satan is the accuser of the brethren. His plan was to get them to doubt God's Word.

If Satan is to defeat you, he must get you to doubt the Word of the Lord. Doubt always causes your faith to fail. Satan understands the power of doubt. Wherever doubt is manifested, fear will be the root. Doubt, which is the same as unbelief, is based in fear. Jesus said on several occasions *"fear not."* He wanted the power of faith to be activated rather than the power of doubt and fear.

As we further our examination of verse five, Satan implies that God is withholding things. *"For God doth know that in the day ye eat thereof, then your eyes shall be opened, and ye shall be as gods, knowing good and evil."* They were already like God; but failed to recognize who they were in God. How many times have you failed to recognize who you are in God?

Many Christians fail to recognize who they are in Christ. In Matthew 4:3, Satan tried to use this same attack against Jesus. His hopes were that Jesus would fail to recognize who He was. Even though he tried, his tactic failed. Why? Jesus knew who He was; the Son of God.

Jesus knew his purpose and had nothing to prove to Satan. Today, he still questions the authority and identity of God's leaders. It is evident, because it is demonstrated on every level of life. Children of every age question the authority of their parents, as well as adults question the authority of leaders. These questions are due to a lack of respect for authority and their identity.

Jesus knew who He was and no tricks or attacks of Satan were going to shake his faith. This is an example of how Christians should exemplify their lives in the body of Christ. We must be confident that whatever promises God has made, He is well able to perform. By developing this attitude, it will cause you to honor the commandments and live by faith.

According to verse five, Satan said, *"then your eyes shall be opened, and ye shall be as gods, knowing good and evil."* After disobeying God, their eyes were opened. This part of Satan's affirmation was true. Their natural eyes were opened from the time of creation; however, the eyes that came opened were their understanding.

Most people believe that they see with their eyes. This is not totally true. Your eyes are windows or an opening to the mind. A greater understanding of this causes us to recognize that we possess optical vision through the brain. The brain receives the image and allows you to perceive what has appeared before the eye. Their understanding or emotional makeup was opened to the things of the world. This allowed them to experience the negative aspects of life. As their lives continued, they were led by the dictates of the flesh.

Verse five indicates Satan made a declaration, *"...and ye shall be as gods, knowing good and evil."* The only thing they knew was they were naked and disobeyed God. To know the difference between good and evil, the Word of God must be taught. This is not knowledge that we automatically possess. Satan wanted them to believe that they would possess knowledge like God.

As we observe the declaration Satan made, I find it to be true, but incomplete. Their knowledge was in-part. Communing with God is the way to receive knowledge of His Word. Some of you are wondering why. In Genesis 2:9, God informed Adam of which trees were good for food, and which were evil. If they were knowledgeable concerning good and evil, God would not have made known the difference. They had to learn the difference between good and evil as we must also learn.

CHAPTER 3
The Results of the Curse

In this chapter, my objective is to reveal the punishment and the results of the absence of the blessing. A negative destination is the result when the blessing is blocked. Let's explore this in greater detail.

> *And the eyes of them both were opened, and they knew that they were naked; and they sewed fig leaves together, and made themselves aprons. And they heard the voice of the Lord God walking in the garden in the cool of the day: and Adam and his wife hid themselves from the presence of the Lord God amongst the trees of the garden. And the Lord God called unto Adam, and said unto him, Where art thou? And he said, I heard thy voice in the garden, and I was afraid, because I was naked; and I hid myself.* (Genesis 3:7-10)

As we explore this passage, it is evident that the blessing was blocked. What do you mean blocked? In Webster's Dictionary, blocked is defined as, *"to stop or make passage difficult."* In other words, the anointing was hindered. Another word for hindered is *"dammed"* which means to block.

After the blessing was blocked or removed, their eyes were opened. They found themselves living by their emotions. A sign that indicates the stimulating of their emotions was: *"they saw their nakedness and hid from the presence of God."* Their willingness to hide indicated a difference in attitude. It also indicates discernment of their disobedience. This is what we do when we disobey God. We try to blame others for our mistakes.

Verse ten denotes that the Lord called him and he replied by saying, *"I heard thy voice in the garden, and I was afraid."* This is where Satan's nature is exemplified. What characteristic of Satan manifested? Fear! Adam experienced fear for the first time in his life. Before they sinned, Adam never experienced fear. He possessed the character of God; love. *"For God hath not given us the spirit of fear; but of power, and of love, and of a sound mind."* (2 Timothy 1:7)

God's punishment to Adam and the woman

In this section, the punishment for disobeying God's command is revealed. Behind every act of disobedience, there is a repercussion. Are you disobeying the commandments? If so, this book will help you to understand the repercussions for disobedience.

I have found that some Christians believe that if Jesus is the Lord of their life, God forgave them of their sins. This is true; nevertheless, there are repercussions for every act of sin. What! Yes! Though God forgave them as He does today through repentance; the seed remains. Let's examine their disobedience and observe how God dealt with sin.

> *Unto the woman he said, I will greatly multiply thy sorrow and thy conception; in sorrow thou shalt bring forth children; and thy desire shall be to thy husband, and he shall rule over thee. And unto Adam he said, Because thou hast hearkened unto the voice of thy wife, and hast eaten of the tree, of which I commanded thee, saying, Thou shalt not eat of it: cursed is the ground for thy sake; in sorrow shalt thou eat of it all the days of thy life; Thorns also and thistles shall it bring forth to thee; and thou shalt eat the herb of the field: In the sweat of thy face shalt thou eat bread, till thou return unto the ground; for out of it wast thou taken: for dust thou art, and unto dust shalt thou return.* (Genesis 3:16-19)

The above passage confirms God's punishment upon Adam and Eve. Though they sinned, these repercussions were appointed by God. They were a result of their disobedience. We must thank God for His superior plan; redemption. God knew that man would fall; thereby, establishing an alternative plan for his redemption.

Adam's disobedience caused his spiritual life to be alienated from God. This gave legal sanction for death. Death is not here by accident. The Bible refers to *"death"* as an enemy. Through Adam's disobedience, death was given legal authorization to fall upon all men. *"Wherefore, as by one man sin entered into the world, and death by sin; and so death passed upon all men, for that all have sinned."* (Romans 5:12)

Satan's Nature Revealed

In Genesis chapter four, the manifestation of Satan's nature is revealed. It is expressed through the life of one of Adam's sons. Cain, Adam's firstborn, was a tiller of the ground, while Abel was a keeper of the sheep. Both sons lived their lives differently. Let's observe the lives of the two brothers and determine who possessed the nature of Satan.

> *And in process of time it came to pass, that Cain brought of the fruit of the ground an offering unto the Lord, And Abel, he also brought of the firstlings of his flock and of the fat thereof. And the Lord had respect unto Abel and to his offering: But unto Cain and to his offering he had not respect. And Cain was very wroth, and his countenance fell.*
>
> (Genesis 4:3-5)

As we observe this passage, it is important to determine why God dishonored Cain's offering. Most ministers use this passage to teach on finances and there is nothing wrong with that concept. Cain, who possessed the nature of Satan exemplified this through his anger. God did not reject his offering but the attitude of his heart. Cain's heart was not right before God. He failed to reconcile with his brother. By failing to reconcile, God denied his offering.

Cain, likened to many Christians today are failing to reconcile with their brothers and sisters. This reconciliation is for both; your spiritual and natural sisters and brothers. Whatever the offense may be, it is your responsibility to reconcile with them. Sometimes people fail to reconcile because an individual would not receive them. It is not your responsibility if the individual does not forgive you. God only requires that you put forth the effort regardless whether the individual ever says anything.

Therefore if thou bring thy gift to the altar, and there rememberest that thy brother hath ought against thee; Leave there thy gift before the altar, and go thy way; first be reconciled to thy brother, and then come and offer thy gift. (Matthew 5:23-24)

God's mercy upon Cain

It is important that we focus in on the love of God. Cain, whose attitude reflects the nature of Satan, is displeased with God and Abel. This was not good and I advise you to examine your heart. Being angry with your brother is one thing but expressing anger towards God can be detrimental. Even though God rejected his offering, He allowed Cain an opportunity of repentance.

Today, some people believe God is waiting on them to sin and cause bad things to happen. This is not God's way of dealing with man. The heart of the Lord is merciful. His desire is that everyone comes to repentance. The heart of the Father is love. As a matter of fact, this is the attitude that Satan does not want you to develop. He knows that if he can get you to develop a wrong attitude towards God, it will not be long before you turn your back on God and begin to live for him. Are you willing to turn your back on God? Don't answer! Please mediate on the question.

As the children of Israel journeyed towards the promise land, some felt the same way. Many rebelled against God because they thought He hated them. This attitude was expressed in Deuteronomy 1:27; *"You complained in your tents and said, The Lord must hate us. That's why he has brought us here from Egypt—to hand us over to the Amorites to be slaughtered."* (*LBT*) This type of attitude made them unwilling to keep God's commands. Therefore, their punishment was a result of a lack of faith. God never punishes his children out of anger, but helps us to see our mistakes.

Genesis 4:7 reveals the hidden revelation. God, who knew the heart of Cain presented him with an opportunity of repentance. The phrase *"if thou doest well"* means, *"to make things well or right with another."* Cain was given the responsibility of making things right with Abel. God informed Cain of the sin that would master his life if he failed to repent.

Cain's failure to honor God's ways of doing and being right led to the path of destruction. *"There is a way which seemeth right unto a man, but the end there of are the ways of death."* (Proverbs 14:12)

Cain left the presence of God and went out after his brother. His heart was filled with jealousy. Instead of correcting his mistake, he gave Satan permission to activate his will and bring death to Abel his brother. Why did Cain permit this? He failed to produce true repentance. By refusing to repent, the seed of jealousy was strengthened. This produced a negative result; death.

As opportunities of repentance are presented, we must repent quickly. For this reason, God called David a man after his own heart; a man who repented quickly. The more we refuse, the longer it takes. This waiting period provides Satan with an opportunity to fortify the seed. As the seed is supported, the situation will magnify. This is one reason we must educate our children and loved ones concerning making right decisions. *"Your life is based in your decisions."* Every decision based on God's way of doing and being right will always produce life. On the other hand, every decision based in fear or your negative emotions produces death.

The blessing upon Noah

God destroyed the earth with a great flood. Noah was his chosen vessel. As life is restored, God finds favor with Noah and empowers him with the anointing. Noah became the first man after the flood to receive the anointing. It's exciting to observe how God blessed him. It was through this empowerment that life was restored upon the earth.

God decided that every living creature must die. This was a result of man's wickedness. God saw the heart of man and knew he would not turn from his wicked ways. Because of this, every living creature, including man and woman, was destroyed. The seed of disobedience was planted in the heart of man. God in his effort to save mankind destroyed the seed of sin.

Although Noah found favor with God, he was instructed to build the Ark. Through his obedience, eight souls were saved. How many souls are you affecting—*whether through positive or negative influence?* God holds us accountable for the lives we influence. We must influence the lives of people in a positive way. Noah, out of his love for God, obeys and builds the Ark.

As time elapsed, Noah remained faithful to God. He and his sons were faithful even in the midst of adversity. This assignment was not easy. The earth had never received rain. Plants and vegetables received their moisture from the dew. Dew is not the same as rain. Have you ever awakened early, went outside your house and observed the dew? This is how plants and vegetables receive water.

Day after day, people passed their work area, speaking evil of them and their work. Some, as they passed by, would call them stupid or foolish. How many times have you tried to do what God instructed you and people constantly ridiculed everything you did? Even though they laugh and call you names, stop and think about Noah. They were building the ark in what we might call the desert. There were no manufacturers, no shopping malls, or anything of such. Only the dry ground with trees and some plants. Regardless of the name calling and the torture they received, Noah and his sons remained faithful to the Lord.

Once the Ark was completed, God gave specific instructions to Noah. The instructions included how the animals should embark upon the Ark. They also included which animals should enter by two (male and female) and the ones by seven. Thank God for the obedience of Noah and his sons. They were sold entirely out to God.

As time passed their wives played an important role in fulfilling their assignment. They did not sit around and watch television or listen to music as some of you may think. They provided support and did whatever they could to comfort their husbands. Their wives were willing to serve at any cost.

Once the Ark was filled, the scène was set. As God instructed Noah to close the door, the rain began. Thousands of human lives and beasts were destroyed. As bad as this sounds, don't think twice about what happened. Only remember that God is merciful.

Finally, after forty days the rain came to an end. After the waters receded, Noah and his family exited the Ark. As time passed, Noah built an altar to the Lord. He worshiped the Lord by offering several of the clean beasts to Him. During the ceremony, God spoke to Noah concerning his will for the earth.

> *And the Lord smelled a sweet savour; and the Lord said in his heart, I will not again curse the ground any more for man's sake; for the imagination of man's heart is evil from his youth; neither will I again smite any more every thing living, as I have done. While the earth remaineth, seedtime and harvest, and cold and heat, and summer and winter, and day and night shall not cease.* (Genesis 8:21-22)

Verse twenty-two is often used concerning finances. This is one of our covenant promises. Thank God for this promise. By possessing the blessing, this promise is available to every Believer. Without a seed, there can be no harvest. So, I encourage you to sow your seeds into good ground.

In exploring the life of Noah, Genesis, chapter nine provides insight of the empowerment upon Noah and his sons. It is important to observe how the blessing affected their lives. A strong indication of the effects of the anointing is revealed in verses one and two. *"And God blessed Noah and his sons, and said unto them, Be fruitful, and multiply, and replenish the earth. And the fear of you and the dread of you shall be upon every beast of the earth, and upon every fowl of the air, upon all that moveth upon the earth, and upon all the fishes of the sea; into your hand are they delivered."* (Genesis 9:1-2)

The above passage indicates that the blessing is an

empowerment from God. Verse one emphasizes the intent and purpose for the anointing. It is here where God gave legal sanction for multiplication. Notice, God spoke multiplication upon Noah and his sons. It was through this family that multiplication occurred. Through this empowerment, Noah and his sons were empowered to rule as Adam.

As we move forward in time, Noah plants a vineyard and becomes drunk. Noah, drunk from wine falls asleep. One of his sons is about to do something that will change the outcome of his entire life. I will not venture into the depths of this story, but will keep my focus on what Noah spoke to his son.

As Noah lay within his tent; suddenly, he was awakened and realized what one of his sons had done to him. Out of anger and embarrassment, he curses one of his sons. Today, many Christians believe that Noah cursed Ham; thereby, leading to the fall of African Americans. However, after a careful examination of the Scriptures, Noah cursed Ham's son Canaan, and not Ham. The curse fell upon his grandson.

> *When Noah awoke from his wine, and knew the thing which his youngest son had done to him, He exclaimed, Cursed be Canaan! He shall be the servant of servants to his brethren!* (Genesis 9:24-25, *AMP*)

According to the Amplified Version, Noah cursed his youngest son. The King James Version says, *"younger son."* In Hebrew, there is no meaning for younger son, but middle son. The two are the same; they both mean grandson. Noah cursed

"Canaan" his grandson. Canaan, Ham's youngest son was cursed by the words of Noah. However, the curse was destroyed as Joshua and the children of Israel entered the Promise Land.

Verse twenty-five indicates that Noah empowered one of his sons. Shem received the blessing from Noah, and he was declared to be blessed of the Lord. It was through this declaration that the blessing rested on him. Please remember this, because as time passes, God searches for another man in whom He can empower with the anointing.

As time passed, Shem died and the blessing had to be located. There is no man in whom God trust with the anointing. It is exciting to discover who God chooses to anoint. Not only is God searching for a man to anoint, but for a bloodline in which Jesus is to enter the world. This bloodline would be special to God. Let's determine who God anoints as his representative.

CHAPTER 4
Abraham; the Chosen Vessel

During this period, the blessing was not upon any man. God continued to search for a vessel that He could empower with the anointing. After many years, God found his chosen vessel. It is through his seed that Christ would be born to a virgin named Mary. *"And Terah lived seventy years, and begat Abram, Nahor, and Haran."* (Genesis 11:26)

The above Scripture denotes that Terah, Abram's father had three sons; Abram being one of the three. God used the bloodline of Abraham to bring Jesus into the world. Verses twenty-nine and thirty indicate that Abram's wife's name was Sarai. The names of Abram's relatives are mentioned with their native land. As time passed, Abram and his relatives left the land of Ur, and lived temporarily in Haran.

As they resided in the land of Haran, the Lord spoke to

Abram concerning his destiny. It is interesting to observe how Abram received the blessing. Abram, a descendant of Shem, found favor with God. However, as a Chaldean, they worshipped such things as idol gods and the moon.

Abram, like most men found himself searching for a greater cause. Have you ever found yourself searching for something that you knew was missing in your life? This is the way Abram felt. He knew within his heart there had to be more than the idol gods they worshipped. Finally, his longing was fulfilled; God spoke to him.

God's promise to Abram

In Genesis chapter twelve, the promise of the blessing is spoken to Abram. Only the promise is mentioned. The empowerment does not occur within this passage. As we continue, I will reveal when and how the empowerment occurred.

> *Now the Lord had said unto Abram, Get thee out of thy country, and from thy kindred, and from thy father's house, unto a land that I will show thee: And I will make of thee a great nation, and I will bless thee, and make thy name great; and thou shalt be a blessing: And I will bless them that bless thee, and curse him that curseth thee: and in thee shall all families of the earth be blessed.* (Genesis 12: 1-3)

Wow! What a powerful promise God gives to Abram. It is Abram's choice whether this promise manifest in his life or not. Most Christians fail to realize that though God speaks his Word, their minds must be renewed. A failure to renew the mind will result in no manifestation.

During this promise, God declared his intended purpose for Abram. This included the establishment of a covenant. What is a covenant? ***"An agreement, usually formal, between two or more persons to do or not do something specified."*** [7] God informed Abram that the promise lies in his faith to believe. This was a covenant of a lifetime. Abram was given the opportunity to become the father of many nations. Chapter fifteen, verse three shows that Abram believed God and by faith he will become the father of many nations.

In verse three, a special promise is mentioned. God declared that all families of the earth will be blessed. The word *"blessed"* is defined as, *"to be empowered."* God's will is for all families to be empowered to prosper. Hamilton agrees by saying, *"The third aspect of the promises made to Abram is concerned with the blessing of those who bless Abram and the cursing of those who curse him, as well as the promise that all families of the earth will be blessed in him"* (12:3).[8]

Some Christians believe and are taught that prosperity is not of God. The entire Bible refers to God prospering His people. As I searched the Scriptures, God constantly speaks about prospering His people. How can prosperity *not* be of God

---

[7] Online Dictionary: www.dictionary.com

[8] James M. Hamilton Jr., "The Seed of the Woman and the Blessing of Abraham," *Tyndale Bulletin* 58, no. 2 (2007): 260.

when He is a God of increase? Hamilton also says, *"The blessing of Abraham promised seed, land, and blessing."*[9] Thank God for the ones who believe and know that God wants them to prosper. Listen to the words of Bowler, *"The American prosperity gospel sanctified a message of more: more faith, more happiness, more health, and more goods to enjoy what God had in store."*[10]

As we observe the life of Abram, his faith was very small. Abram, like Believers today, had to learn to trust God. This is not an overnight process. It takes time to develop a relationship with God. This is where some Christians fail; not knowing how to wait on the Lord. As Christians, there is a course of development that we must endure to perfect our faith. Abram believed and trusted God even during adversities.

As we reflect on Genesis 12:1, Abram's first test was to leave his country. This included his father's house, relatives, and associates. It also included anyone having negative influence on his life. How many of you would leave your country or family because God instructed you? If you said, *"I would"* without having any hesitations, I encourage you to examine your faith.

Abram did not leave in the way many of you might think. I believe he pondered on the Word of the Lord before moving forward. His pondering was an indication of a lack of faith. How many of you can relate to this? Abram, like many

---

[9] Ibid., 272.

[10] Kate Bowler, and Wen Reagan, "Bigger, Better, Louder: The Prosperity Gospel's Impact on Contemporary Christian Worship," *Religion and American Culture* 24, no. 2 (2014): 192.

Christians today, had no relationship with God. He had to learn to trust God at his word.

Most Christians today constantly hear about faith. Faith without understanding will surely fail. Many of you can attest to this. How many times have you tried operating in faith only to find things getting worse? This is where we blame God by saying, *"that faith stuff doesn't work."* God is not the one who failed. Failure lies in your lack of understanding. As Abram's relationship grew in the Lord, his faith grew. His faith and trust in God caused him to become a friend of God.

Abram Leaves for the Promise Land

After God made His promise to Abram, Abram left for the land of Canaan. As he journeyed toward Canaan, he passed through several cities and built altars unto the Lord. As Abram erected each altar, his prayers increased. This strengthened his relationship. Finally, he continued his journey towards Egypt where famine permeated the land.

As he entered Egypt, God granted Abram favor with Pharaoh. Some of Pharaoh's soldiers immediately captured them and began to inquire of their journey. Out of fear, Abram and Sarai lied to the Egyptians by saying they were brother and sister. Sarai was immediately restrained by the Egyptians who escorted her into Pharaoh's house. Though this happened, God's favor was exemplified through Sarai. What the devil meant for evil, God worked out for their good.

He is doing the same thing today. He is constantly working on our behalf concerning the things that Satan has orchestrated for evil and turning them into good. Many of these things we have brought upon ourselves by making decisions that were not of God. Thank God that He is merciful.

It amazes me how God was in control. Though the situation was bad, God remained in control. When you obey Him, and follow his commands, He goes before you making your enemies to be at *"peace."* The word *"peace"* is defined in the Hebrew as, *"Shalom."* Shalom is defined as, *"peace or prosperity."* God not only gives you peace of mind but causes your enemies to bless you. *"And he entreated Abram well for her sake: and he had sheep, and oxen, and he asses, and menservants, and maidservants, and she asses, and camels."* (Genesis 12:16) This is a result of the steps of a good man being ordered by the Lord, and he delights in his way. (Psalm 37:23)

This is a preview of what God does when we obey *Him*. He is waiting to prosper his children. The blessing empowers you to do everything God intends. Abram accomplished this task without possessing the anointing. The material blessings were a result of his obedience. Even after reading and observing how God blessed Abram, many Christians continue to have problems with prosperity.

As time passed, war broke out among several kings. These kings are mentioned in Genesis 14:1-2. I will not expound upon the war, but will reveal how Abram rescued Lot in the midst of adversity. Abram possessed a greater defense than his adversary. He had God on his side and God made the difference. In verse twelve, the enemy captured Lot. He was imprisoned, and his possessions were seized by the enemy.

Abram immediately sought God's counsel. He was determined not to simply pray, but added faith with his prayers. How many times have you sat back and waited on God and nothing happened? In modern life, this happens day after day. Christians constantly pray but fail to add corresponding actions to their prayers. God is a God of faith. Without adding corresponding actions to your prayers, how can they be honored? Time after time I have seen Christians pray for God to do something in their lives but they fail to add corresponding actions. Faith is not believing only; but adding actions that are equivalent to your beliefs.

Dr. Dollar says faith is, *"Your response to what God has already done."*[11] To give you a better understanding, I will illustrate an example of faith.

Once, a church held a revival in the desert. I know this sounds ridiculous but remain patient and receive the understanding. As the revival was held, several men from different states and countries attended. One day, a young man traveled through the desert to attend the service. As he traveled, suddenly, his car stalled. Not knowing what to do, he immediately began to walk toward his destination.

---

[11] Dollar, Faith and Grace.

As he journeyed, he became exhausted and fatigue began over-taking his mind. Though exhaustion had an effect on him, he made his way to the revival. As he approached, he stumbled and several men ran to assist him. Immediately, they brought the young man into the sanctuary and began to examine him. One of the brothers, a doctor, informed the young man that he was dehydrated. After careful examination, they placed a glass of water before him. As the young man received enough strength to talk, he began to say, *"If I drink this water, I shall live and not die."* This he did several times. However, after repeating this phrase, he failed to drink the water and died.

Let's observe what happened. First, the young man exhausted from his travel was examined and informed of his condition. Secondly, the doctor specifically informed him of his dehydration. Even though a glass of water was set before him, instead of drinking, he continued to recite: *"If I drink this water, I shall live and not die."* This was all completely true. However, his greatest mistake was likened to many Believers today; he failed to add corresponding actions with his belief. His failure to drink the water (provided by God), led to his untimely death.

Now, do you see how faith requires corresponding actions? I know that many of you have heard and even some taught that all you need is a little faith. This sounds good but it's incomplete. This is not scriptural! You may believe; but, if you fail to add corresponding actions to your belief, the result is failure. Abram demonstrated to Believers how to walk in faith.

Through his faith, God delivered him and rescued Lot.

Abram meets Melchizedek

In this subchapter, I'll reveal the empowerment upon Abram. This empowerment was established through the covenant promise; *"in thee shall all families of the earth be blessed."* In our previous chapter, Abram encountered an overwhelming victory against his enemies. The victory set the stage for the empowerment upon Abram's life.

> *And Melchizedek king of Salem brought forth bread and wine: and he was the priest of the most high God. And he blessed him, and said Blessed be Abram of the most high God, possessor of heaven and earth: And blessed be the most high God, which hath delivered thine enemies into thy hand. And he gave him tithes of all.* (Genesis 14:18-20)

In this passage, Abram meets Melchizedek. It is important to determine what happened between the two men. If we determine the importance of their meeting and its benefits, we'll understand the transference of the anointing. To reach this understanding, we must first understand who Melchizedek was and the vital role he played in Abram's life.

> *For this Melchisedec, king of Salem, priest of the most high God, who met Abraham returning from the slaughter of the kings, and blessed him; To whom also Abraham gave a tenth part of all; first being by interpretation King of righteousness, and after that also*

> *King of Salem, which is, King of peace; Without father, without mother, without descent, having neither beginning of days, nor end of life; but made like unto the Son of God; abideth a priest continually.* (Hebrews 7:1-3)

According to Granerod, "*For the historian Josephus, Melchizedek is a thoroughly human figure — he is seen as a Canaanite and the first one to have built a temple (Bell. 6,438).*"[12] Upon further examination, we see that Melchizedek was a representative of God. He represented the Most High. He was the risen *Shem*.

McNamara says, "*The name* מלכי־צדק *is reproduced in Tg. Onq. and in Frg. Tgs. PVNL. Tg. Ps.-J. has* מלכא צדיקא*,*" *the righteous king — in full: 'the righteous king, he is Shem son of Noah, king of Jerusalem'*".[13] How can this be? When Shem, a descendant of Noah died, the blessing remained on him. There was no one designated by God to receive the anointing. This allowed the blessing to remain upon him even in death. This sounds odd, but it's true.

> *And Elisha died, and they buried him. And the bands of the Moabites invaded the land at the coming in of the year. And it came to pass, as they were burying a man, that, behold, they spied a band of men; and they cast the man into the sepulchre of Elisha: and when the*

---

[12] Gard Granerød, "Melchizedek in Hebrews 7," *Biblical* 90, no. 2 (2009): 196.
[13] Martin McNamara, "Melchizedek: Gen 14,17-20 in the Targums, in Rabbinic and Early Christian Literature," *Biblica* 81, no. 1 (2000): 8.

man was let down, and touched the bones of Elisha, he revived, and stood up on his feet. (2 Kings 13:20-21)

The above Scripture speaks of Shem being transformed into Melchizedek. According to this passage, a dead man was revived at the point of contact. As his body touched the anointing on the bones of Elisha, he was revived. Notice where the anointing lied; on the bones of Elisha who was dead. Now, if the anointing can revive a dead man, I have no doubt that God, who is *"Superior,"* touched Shem's body and empowered him to appear as Melchizedek.

It is important to remember that Jesus would come through the bloodline of Abraham. Shem is a descendant of Noah and Abraham is a descendant of Shem. The bloodline was set. God knew exactly how to accomplish His purpose.

Now that we have a greater understanding of Melchizedek, we gain a greater revelation. Melchizedek, a forerunner of Christ, was the first coming of Jesus. It was through the order of Melchizedek that Jesus was made our High Priest. *"Where Jesus has entered in for us [in advance], a Forerunner having become a High Priest forever after the order (with the rank) of Melchizedek."* (Hebrews 6:20, *AMP*)

Melchizedek represented God as [High Priest] and blessed Abram. As they assembled in Abram's tent, communion was administered. During communion, Melchizedek spoke to Abram concerning his victory. He reminded Abram that God delivered his enemies into his hands and without God, there would be no victory. This caused Abram to envision himself as he once was; without God.

As Abram examined his heart, he realized without God he would have lost the battle. By realizing this, he made a decision that changed his entire life. He decided to honor the Lord with his tithes. What a good decision to make! Through this decision, the exchange was made. What exchange? As Abram blessed Melchizedek with the tithes, Melchizedek empowered him with the blessing. This was the exchange.

The exchange of the tithes is key to possessing the blessing. Abram realized that without God he would not have the wealth he possessed or won the battle. Abram realized that he owed God. The releasing of the tithes was a token of his love. Love is the key. You cannot truly love the Lord without loving Him with your possessions.

Abram gave of the tithes and Melchizedek blessed (empowered) Abram. The blessing now rested on Abram. In the upcoming chapter, we will explore the blessing in greater depths. Every Believer has a right to the blessing. Satan knows and understands the power of the anointing. As Christians, we must educate ourselves on the blessing and permit it to flow in every area of our lives.

How the blessing affected Abram

In Genesis 15:1-4, God appeared to Abram after his empowerment. His first Word were: *"Fear not."* God spoke these words with the intent to let Abram know that he could trust

Him. The presence of fear would have caused him to abort the Word of the Lord. As God approached, He wanted Abram to have peace of mind and receive the Word of Life.

Now that Abram possesses the anointing, Satan immediately brings the spirit of fear. One of Satan's tricks as usual was to get Abram to distrust God. Immediately, God announced that He was his shield and exceeding great reward. God informed Abram that He was his source. Everything Abram needed was in Him. God would be his revenue or whatever he desired Him to be. Let's examine Abram's first request.

Abram's first request included something most Christians fail to ask because they lack faith. They know that God can perform but realizes their faith is weak. Abram's request was realistic. The blessing was the key to the manifestation. *"And Abram said, Behold, to me thou hast given no seed: and, lo, one born in my house is mine heir."* (Genesis 15:3)

Abram's request involved having a seed. Having a son is likened to the difference between day and night. He knew God would have to prove Himself by providing a seed. To a man, producing a seed (child) is everything. The question in most people's mind is: can the blessing produce positive results? The answer to this question is yes.

In Deuteronomy 8:18, God reminded his people that He empowered them to get wealth. The empowerment is the blessing. Wealth is not just money but whatever you need to live the prosperous life. It could be finances for one person; healing to another; or deliverance for all. It makes no difference; God has empowered us with the ability (anointing) to possess what we need in life. In Abram's situation, the anointing produced life in a barren situation.

If life is to exist, there must be a Word from the Lord. He is the life-giver. Without God, there is no life and nothing can exist. Many of you walk around day after day without living. You walk around alive, but you don't live. To live the God-abundant life, you must be born again and filled with the Holy Spirit. This is what life is all about. Abram needed God to breathe life into his situation. There are times today when we need God to breathe life into our situations. Without life, only death exists; and death is the absence of God.

Sarai had no relationship with God. During this time, God communed only with Abram. Just as many wives today must learn to trust the words of their husbands, Sarai had to do the same. Please remember that God communicated with Abram. Consequently, she had to trust the words of her husband. Regardless of their present situation, they had to trust God.

In Genesis 15:4, God spoke to Abram concerning his future heir. The Word of the Lord was released and received by Abram. God gave specific instructions concerning the seed. How Abram valued the word would be the difference in having a descendant or Sarai remaining barren. Their future rested in the hands of Abram's faith.

After receiving the word, Abram immediately informed Sarai. It is important to recognize the mindset of Sarai as she hears the words of Abram. How did she value his words? Wives, how do you value the words of your husband? Do you hear what they say or do you insist on having your way? Please mediate on this!

Some of you may ask, *"why Abram's words?"* Simple. God spoke to him. Abram became responsible for communicating the word to Sarai. The promised child depended on her willingness to receive the words of Abram. This is exactly what happened to Adam. God spoke to him but it was his responsibility to communicate what God said to Eve, his wife. Do you see the importance of communication?

As he communicated the Word of the Lord to Sarai, she failed to receive his words. She did not want to hear what Abram had to say. She rejected the Word of the Lord. Sarai, who was filled with rejection because of her barrenness, implemented her own plan. It is here where Abram failed to use his authority and created an avenue for her plans. Sarai overstepped her boundary and operated in the role of her husband. This was totally out of order. The order of God was broken just as it was with Adam and Eve.

In our society, the order of God concerning the covenant union of marriage is often broken. Most often, it is due to a lack of understanding authority. Women, be careful when it comes to making decisions. Yes, every couple needs to sit down and communicate concerning situations; however, after careful consideration, the last words should be that of your husband. It is the husband's responsibility to take the situation before God and receive his way of doing and being right. This will eliminate confusion and every evil work.

> *But there is one thing I want you to know: The head of every man is Christ, the head of woman is man, and the head of Christ is God.* (1 Corinthians 11:3, *NLT*)

The above Scripture states that the man is the head of his wife. The man (husband in Christ) is definitely the head. Sarai assumed Abram's role and forced her will upon their lives. Abram failed to execute his authority agreeing with the plan of Sarai. This plan included more than the two of them, but another life. Hagar, the handmaid of Sarai obeyed and agreed to the terms of her mistress. It was out of this plan that Ishmael was born. Let's examine how Sarai's way of doing effected their lives.

God told Abram in Genesis 15:4, *"but he that shall come forth out of thine own bowels shall be thine heir."* Abram failed to get understanding concerning the word. His lack of understanding led to a negative result. Sarai, felt betrayed by Hagar, the Egyptian, who knew that she was the mother of Abram's first born. Hagar allowed the spirit of pride to enter her heart. This created an attitude of selfishness. Meanwhile, Sarai continues to feel betrayed by Hagar and places a demand on Abram.

She immediately demanded Abram to remove Hagar from her presence. This is a result of what happens when we initiate our own will. At this point, Sarai could not stand the thought of knowing that Hagar was the rightful mother. Day after day, she flirted in her face rubbing it in that she was the mother. Finally, Sarai realized that she failed to believe the words of her husband. Abram's failure was due to a lack of faith. A lack of understanding will always produce a lack of faith.

In Mark 4:23-24, Jesus spoke about the importance of hearing. According to Jesus, hearing is essential. Understanding is produced through hearing. Your ability to hear *"intelligently"* produces positive results. Abram failed to ponder appropriately concerning this matter. He failed to receive clarity about the situation. Think about it; how many times have you rushed out to do something because someone spoke a word to you or you heard God. Though this may be true, it remains your responsibility to receive clarity before moving forward.

Verse twenty-four denotes the man who hears intelligently. To him more will be given. As we ponder the word, God reveals things to do. This produces the faith to carry out what is said. Once again this is where most Christians fail concerning faith. We fail to wait on God and find his way of doing and being right.

Abram failed to receive clarity on what God spoke. Therein lies the problem. He never possessed the wisdom of God. He assumed by his own bowel (not including Sarai) would a child be born. In other words, when God said, *"through your bowels,"* He was referring to them. God saw them as one and not two twains. It is through our inability to hear that problems arise. Abram's inability to hear intelligently produced an Ishmael. The name Ishmael refers to *"wild man."*

Time has passed and Abram is eighty-six years old. Ishmael is on the scene. Hagar and Ishmael are forced to leave and live elsewhere. The Lord is with her and promises to bless Ishmael. Thirteen more years have passed and Abram is ninety-nine years old. During this period, God refrained from speaking allowing Abram to evaluate his mistakes. In other words, this was the time for Abram to mature in his faith. Thank God that He permits time for us to develop.

In Genesis 17:1, Abram's faith has matured and God speaks to him. How is your faith? Has your faith matured? If you are having a hard time hearing from God, you need to stay in his presence. Spend time in the Word of God and your faith will develop. Developing your godly relationship strengthens your faith. The word that God released transformed Abram's entire life.

> *I will make a covenant with you, by which I will guarantee to give you countless descendants." At this, Abram fell face down on the ground. Then God said to him, "This is my covenant with you: I will make you the father of a multitude of nations! What's more, I am changing your name. It will no longer be Abram.*

Instead, you will be called Abraham, for you will be the father of many nations. (Genesis 17:2-5, *NLT*)

God confirmed His word which He spoke in Genesis 12:2. God made a covenant with Abram. The covenant included changing his name. No longer would he be known as Abram, but Abraham. God renamed him because of his intended purpose for man. As God observed Abram's faith, He declared that he would be the one by which all families of the earth would be blessed. This covenant made the blessing available to all Believers.

The covenant was established and ready to be enforced. Only one problem remained; Abram had no seed. According to the covenant, a seed was promised to him. *"And I will establish my covenant between me and thee and thy seed after thee in their generations for an everlasting covenant, to be a God unto thee, and to thy seed after thee."* (Genesis 17:7)

This Scripture shows that Abram was promised a seed. I will not expound on the revelation but will reveal it later. According to the covenant, a child is mentioned. Sarai received a word from the Lord that transformed her entire life. In Genesis 17:15-16, God made known to Abraham his intended purpose. As God's will was revealed, Abraham became fearful. He questioned God's ability to perform his word. Thank God, the question was justifiable. God ignored his stupidity and provided the name of the promise child. Abraham was to call his son Isaac.

As time passed, the Lord appeared to Abraham in the

plains of Mamre. In the heat of the day, three men (Theophanies) approached and communed with him. During communion, they spoke concerning Isaac. Here is where God confirmed His word. Finally, Sarah conceived and Isaac was born. It was during this time as Isaac grew, Hagar and Ishmael were forced to leave. Isaac, the promise child continued to grow while Abraham pondered the covenant.

Before the blessing was transferred upon Isaac, God tested Abraham's faith once again. Through this test of faith, Jesus would come and fulfill the covenant. Abraham's faith was on the line. The test included Isaac. If Jesus is to come through this test, we need to know how God challenged Abraham's faith.

In Genesis 22:1-12, God tried Abraham's faith by asking him to sacrifice his son. My question to you is how would you feel if God asked you to sacrifice your son; especially, if he is your only son? The answer to this question will be different in the hearts and minds of every Believer. However, Abraham was confronted with this awesome test. The Bible states that after three days he saw the place which God instructed him to go. Though three days had passed, Abraham obeyed God.

As they journeyed towards Mount Moriah, Isaac followed his father. The two of them carried the wood, knife, and fire used in the sacrifice. As they approached Moriah, Isaac questioned his father concerning the sacrifice. Immediately, Abraham reminded Isaac that God would provide. Abraham was not going to permit fear to grip their minds resulting in doubt and unbelief. This is how Christians should approach any situation that arises in their lives. Abraham casted down imaginations and negative thoughts that tried to exalt themselves above the Word of God.

Finally, they reached the place of sacrifice. Isaac, in obedience to Abraham, laid upon the altar. Out of reverence to God, Abraham proceeded to accomplish his mission. Through this test of obedience, an angel of the Lord called out from Heaven to Abraham. He assured him of his love for God. How many of you would love for an angel to reassure you of your love for God? I believe the angel gave Abraham the confidence that God was well-pleased with his faith. Then, he turned and fastened his eyes upon the ultimate sacrifice; a lamb caught in a bush. Through this sacrifice, God proclaimed the fullness of the covenant upon him.

God reminds Abraham of His promise

Abraham proved faithful to the very end of his task. Isaac's willingness to trust his father made the assignment tolerable. In Genesis 22:16-18, God rewarded Abraham by making an oath that could not be broken. It was through this vow that we are blessed today. The covenant speaks for itself. What a promise to make! Abraham obeyed God and the blessing is now made available to all Believers.

And said, I have sworn by Myself, says the Lord, that since you have done this and have not withheld [from Me] or begrudged [giving Me] your son, your only son, In blessing I will bless you and in multiplying I will multiply your descendants like the stars of the heavens and like the sand on the seashore. And your Seed (Heir) will possess the gate of His enemies, And in your Seed [Christ] shall all the nations of the earth be blessed and [by Him] bless themselves, because you have heard and obeyed My voice. (Genesis 22:16-18, *AMP*)

As we look closer at the covenant, verse seventeen emphasizes the extent of the covenant. God declared prosperity upon Abraham and his descendants. His seed would be likened to the stars of heaven and the sand upon the seashore. What a remarkable covenant to possess. Not only would Abraham benefit from this covenant, but his descendants.

As time continued to pass, Abraham became old in age and the Lord blessed him in all things. Sarah his former wife is dead. Abraham remarried and received a wife whose name was Keturah. Several sons were born from this union. Abraham is now at the point of death. Before he dies, the blessing must be transferred to Isaac. In the upcoming chapter, I will reveal how the blessing was transferred to Isaac and how it impacted his life.

CHAPTER 5
The Blessing Upon Isaac

In the previous chapter, Abraham was at the point of death. The blessing remains upon him, but must be transferred upon Isaac. The promise seed of Abraham is in place and God allows him to transfer his anointing upon Isaac. As we observe the life of Isaac, let's examine how the blessing affected his life.

And Abraham gave all that he had unto Isaac. (Genesis 25:5) This is where the transference occurred. Dennis Sylva depicts Isaac as, *". . . a little man governed by little goals with little closeness to bequeath to the next generation."*[14] Isaac received the anointing while the sons of the concubines received gifts. The blessing is now upon Isaac. He received the root to the fruit. Isaac received the blessing which empowered his entire

---

[14] Dennis Sylva, "The Blessing of a Wounded Patriarch: Genesis 27.1-40," *Journal for the Study of the Old Testament* 32, no. 3 (March 2008): 273.

life.

According to Sylva, *"The blessing is a defining event that will convey what is essential about Isaac's life."*[15] The sons of the concubines received their portion as material gifts. Gifts are not the same as the blessing. Material gifts, even though some are extravagant, are given by man; but the anointing is given by God. However, death comes to Abraham.

Abraham is dead and Isaac must live as his father did. The anointing has changed his life. As we study his life, the effects of the blessing are exemplified. Let's explore whether the anointing prospered Isaac as it did Abraham. In Genesis 26, a famine developed in the land. This famine was identical to the famine during the life of Abraham. Isaac, because of the famine matriculated to Gerar.

As he journeyed, the Lord appeared to him in a vision instructing Isaac not to go to Egypt, but to reside in Gerar. During this time, God declared His covenant to Isaac and tested his faith. As Isaac obeyed God, He spoke concerning the covenant. Isaac's faith was tested in the same manner as Abraham's. As they entered the city of Gerar, some of the men inquired of Rebekah. Isaac found himself doing just as Abraham did previously. He asked Rebekah to lie for him. This was exactly what Sarai did for Abram. Rebekah obeyed and did as requested. Meanwhile, the men of Gerar refused to hear their words and escorted Rebekah to Abimelech.

---

[15] Ibid., 268.

After residing in Gerar for a period of time, Abimelech noticed the two of them sporting with each other. This was perfectly alright in one sense because they were married. Many times, this is exemplified in the lives of couples today; especially, those whose husbands or wives are incarcerated. As they greet each other, intimate feelings are expressed. Those who truly love each other have a higher level of intimacy expressed than those who are not married. Regardless, the truth was hiding from the king.

The word sporting implies, *"expressing intimate feelings."* Their feelings expressed actions beyond that of brotherly love. This led Abimelech to inquire of their relationship. Finally, they admitted their faults and were forgiven by the king. Listen to the words of Victor H. Matthews, *"If nothing else, the "wife-sister" deception did operate as a means whereby Abraham and Isaac separately acquired substantial wealth (in terms of larger herds and a larger number of servants)."*[16]

Forgiveness is one of the keys to answered prayers. As God granted them favor with Abimelech, he made a declaration before the people concerning them. The favor of the Lord was exemplified through the declaration. The declaration not only reflected the favor of God but the fear of the Lord. The words of Abimelech changed the attitude of the people. The declaration provided the same respect for Isaac and Rebekah as it did for

---

[16] Victor H. Matthews, "The Wells of Gerar," *Biblical Archaeologist* 49, no. 2 (June 1986): 122.

Abimelech. Meanwhile, Isaac began to sow seeds into the parched ground where God would demonstrate his magnificent power.

> *"Then Isaac sowed in that land, and received in the same year an hundredfold: and the Lord blessed him."* (Genesis 26:12)

Isaac sowed into the common ground of Gerar. Though this is true, I believe there is a greater revelation. This Scripture can be viewed as twofold. A greater revelation reveals that Isaac sowed into the life of Abimelech. This act was symbolic to what Abram did with Melchizedek. Isaac realized that God turned Abimelech's heart from destroying him. Broadening your understanding, this Scripture provides one word that refers to the two-fold; *"then."*

The word *"then"* implies a period of time. This time-frame allowed Isaac to reflect on the mercy of God. Through meditation, Isaac realized God delivered him and Rebekah from the wrath of Abimelech. Therefore, Isaac [just as Abram gave to Melchizedek] sowed into the life of Abimelech. As he sowed into Abimelech, he was given to God.

Some of you wonder how this can be. Abimelech operated in the highest power in Gerar. He was the King! The power he possessed was of God. Isaac sowed into the anointing and God blessed him. Whose anointing are you sowing into? Do you have a man or woman of God or ministry to whom you sow seeds? If not, I advise you to pray and ask God to show you your leader.

Isaac, who was led by the Spirit of God, sowed into the parched soil. Though the ground was unfit for planting and no rain had fallen, God honored his faith. This is the second part of the twofold Scripture. Isaac sowed spiritually, then physically, and God blessed the seed. Some of you may question, how can this be? Isaac released his faith by sowing into the life of Abimelech. It makes no difference how much faith you confess to have, if you fail to release it, no manifestation [nothing] will be the result. Faith without works is dead.

Isaac sowed and God prospered the works of his hands. His success was a result of his obedience. Isaac demonstrated to all Believers how to trust God during famine. This example is for all Christians to respect and to learn. Obedience is the key to releasing your faith. Isaac released his faith and God grew the seed. Sowing financially is another key to a successful life.

As we conclude this section, Isaac became extremely rich. For those who think prosperity is not of God, the life of Abraham and Isaac represents the covenant of prosperity. God delights in us when we prosper. As Isaac prospered, the Philistines envied him. His success was beyond measure. He prospered so much until his enemies, the Philistines, forced him to leave. Matthews says, *"Because the growth of Isaac's herds and his agricultural activity may have already overtaxed the available local water supply, no other migrants could be allowed to settle here. Such a situation would also provide a practical basis for the command that Isaac and his herds depart the area of Gerar."*[17]

Today, not only do Christians have problems with prosperity, but non-Christians as well. If you are wealthy and have not confessed Christ, then the world thinks that it is alright for you to be wealthy. I have observed the attitude of the world towards those who are born-again and wealthy; it is unjust. Why would God, who owns everything, [includes everything you possess] withhold wealth from his own?

Fathers, who love their children and desire to see them live the best life, would they not do everything in their power to provide a better life for them. If you are saying yes, how can God, who loves us all do any less? It makes no difference if you are born-again or not; God is a just God. He allows his rain to fall on the unrighteous as well as the righteous. He is the maker of them all.

---

[17] Ibid.

CHAPTER 6
Jacob Receives the Blessing

"Therefore, God give thee of the dew of heaven, and the fatness of the earth, and plenty of corn and wine: Let people serve thee, and nations bow down to thee: be lord over thy brethren, and let thy mother's sons bow down to thee: cursed be every one that curseth thee, and blessed be he that blesseth thee." (Genesis 27:28-29)

Isaac has grown older and desires to bless Esau and Jacob. A customary tradition was the eldest son received the inheritance of his father. Jacob, whose name means supplanter, tricked his brother and received his birthright. As you continue to read, I'll reveal how Jacob received the birthright from Esau. Today, the word "birthright" is rarely mentioned, and has no significance among the sons of men.

The birthright is everything to a son. This traditional

covenant enabled the firstborn to receive a double portion of his father's inheritance and to carry the name of the family. Both Esau and Jacob understood the importance of the birthright. However, I caution you to hear the words of Ruben Ahroni who says, *"References to primogeniture in Ancient Eastern records clearly indicate, as E. A. Speiser and others have shown, that the primacy of birth was a matter of the father's discretion, irrespective of chronological priority."*[18] In other words, the father had the right to give the birthright to the younger son if so desired.

Today, most fathers fail to educate their sons concerning their inheritance. A reason for this could be that most fail to possess the blessing; thereby, depriving their sons of their inheritance. As we further our understanding, it becomes obvious as to what Jacob did to possess the birthright. Jacob, a plain man; *"one with fewer gifts or talents,"* decided to make lentil stew. As he prepared the pottage, Esau tired from hunting asked him for a portion of the stew. Being fatigued, Esau exaggerated his exhaustion, and Jacob took advantage of him.

As Esau elaborated, Jacob demanded him to sell his birthright. Being exhausted and hungry, Esau failed to discern the motives of his brother. His failure caused him to relinquish all rights to his birth. Ahroni expounds more on the birthright by saying:

---

[18] Reuben Ahroni, "Why did Esau Spurn the Birthright: A Study in Biblical Interpretation," *Judaism* 29, no. 3 (1980): 323.

"What is remarkable is the narrative of the Jacob-Esau episode is not the mere transfer of the birthright from the elder to the younger. Rather it is the fact that, in this specific case, primogeniture was treated like any merchandise, subject to purchase through an agreement between the parties concerned—the seller and the buyer. And indeed, this transfer of the birthright from Esau to Jacob is conducted like an ordinary commercial transaction. Esau literally barters away his birthright. Moreover, this transaction is assumed to be valid even without the father's sanction or knowledge."[19]

Jacob's motive was to use the birthright against Esau should Isaac bless him. During this time, Jacob did not know the will of God. His actions were expressed out of fear. Therefore, his aspiration was for him. However, Rebekah, Jacob's mother knew the will of God for her sons. During her pregnancy, God spoke to her concerning the destiny of the two boys. She knew precisely what their destiny held. Her only concern was how this could be. We must remember that with God all things are possible. God is faithful to his Word and it will not return void.

One day, Rebekah overheard Isaac speaking to Esau concerning the blessing. His request was for Esau to go hunting and afterwards, make his favorite meal. Now Isaac loved Esau while Rebekah loved Jacob. Sylva described the relationship between Isaac and his sons by saying, "We read that he loves

---

[19] Ibid., 324.

Esau, but never that he loves Jacob."[20] Though they both loved their sons, favoritism was exemplified.

Favoritism should never be exemplified within a family. It leads to division and causes strife. Isaac, out of love for Esau, desired to anoint him with the blessing. Sylva also depicts Isaac's love for Esau as he says, *"His love for Esau is, however, the result of the savory food that the skillful hunter Esau procures and prepares for him (25.28a). Even the final blessing that, at the end of Isaac's life, he wants to bestow on Esau is tied to his love of the food that Esau brings."*[21] This was not the will of God for Esau. Meanwhile, Rebekah pondered on the Word of the Lord.

I believe God revealed His will to Rebekah because He knew that Isaac, out of love for Esau [firstborn], would desire to follow his traditional family heritage. This is a perfect example of how tradition operates in the minds of people. Isaac, leaning to his own way of thinking, failed to seek God for the destiny of the two boys. This is where most fathers fail.

Tradition becomes a strong part of our decisions. We feel as though things must remain the same. Isaac knew the birthright belonged to the eldest son, and he was not about to change. This caused his thinking to be out of the will of God.

As time passed, Esau was out in the field while Jacob disguised himself to be Esau. As Jacob approached Isaac, his

---

[20] Sylva, The Blessing of a Wounded Patriarch, 270.
[21] Ibid.

presence was questioned. Isaac, who was at the point of permanent blindness, was totally led by his emotions. Because of his blindness, he smelled Jacob and listened carefully to his voice to discern if he was Esau. The plan of Rebekah worked. Isaac blessed Jacob, and he received the blessing. The will of God was accomplished, and Rebekah was overwhelmed to see the plan of God fulfilled. This caused her heart to be at peace with God.

As Isaac blessed Jacob, financial prosperity is mentioned. According to the words of Isaac, he spoke primarily of natural things. Such things included *"the fatness of the earth, corn and wine."* These natural substances indicate that God's blessings include more than spiritual blessings. The blessing also includes material goods. This is also an area of life where some Christians have problems with material wealth. Isaac mentioned material goods and God blessed Jacob exceedingly. To think that God blesses you only with spiritual gifts would be denying yourself of everything the covenant of prosperity offers. Please stop and mediate on this!

Esau obeyed his father and prepared his favorite dinner. Upon his return, he was too late. Jacob had supplanted his brother twice. He acquired the blessing and fled for his life. As Esau approached his father, he realized that Isaac blessed Jacob instead of him. This caused Esau to become angry and filled with hatred. The following Scripture reflects the attitude of both Isaac and Esau towards Jacob.

And he said, Thy brother came with subtlety, and hath taken away thy blessing. And he said, Is not he rightly named Jacob? For he hath supplanted me these two times: he took away my birthright; and, behold, now he hath taken away my blessing. And he said, hast thou not reserved a blessing for me? (Genesis 27:35-36)

Rebekah's way did not appear to be right; however, God was in the midst. Jacob's willingness to trust his mother enabled him to possess the blessing. There are times when we do things in an unusual manner. However, this may be the way of the Lord. Leaning to your own understanding causes failures. To prevent these failures, we must acknowledge God in all our ways.

The Blessing upon Jacob

In this section, we will observe the blessing upon Jacob. Esau realizes that he is his brother's servant and anger fills his heart. Jacob, who is knowledgeable of his brother's anger, flees for his life. How many of you have felt the way Esau feels? His negative feelings dictated to him. He had to take authority over them and walk in the mind of Christ.

As we observe the life of Jacob, the effects of the blessing manifested in his life. Jacobs' life is a perfect example of the how the blessing flows. Without the blessing, his life would have been unproductive. Let's examine the effects of the blessing, and how it affected his life and the lives of others.

In *Genesis 28*, Jacob is instructed by Isaac to receive a

wife. Now Abraham and his descendants believed in covenant marriage, "Endogamy." *"Endogamy involved marriage within a specific tribe or similar social unit."* No other culture, nationality, or religion was acceptable. Jacob J. Weinstein described the importance of Canaanite marriage as, *"A third party, Eliezer, precursor of the modern shadchan, selects Rebekah as the right mate for the son of his master because she stems from the same family background, the same social caste, and would therefore be the more likely to fit into the kind of life which Isaac would be bound to live."*[22] For this reason was Jacob instructed to receive a wife from his uncle, Laban.

Laban is the brother of Rebekah; Jacob's mother. This traditional covenant was established within the lineage of Abraham. Laban had several daughters and Jacob's wife lie in the midst. Jacob finds himself being obedient and journeys towards Padan-aram, the house of Laban. As he obeyed Isaac, Esau waited patiently to avenge his brother. Remember, Esau was highly upset with Jacob. Hatred filled his heart, and he was determined to get even with his brother.

Jacob's Dream

As Jacob traveled towards the house of Laban, he became weary from his journey. As he gathered stones for his pillows, sleep and exhaustion overtook his physical strength.

---

[22] Jacob J. Weinstein, "Isaac and Rebekah: The Jewish Conception of Love and Marriage as Compared with the Western Romantic Tradition," *The Reconstructionist* 15, no. 8 (May 27, 1949): 9.

While he slept, he fell into a deep sleep and began to dream. In his dream, the Lord appeared to him revealing his will for his life. Today, the power of dreams is rarely understood.

As Jacob awakes, he realizes that God revealed his future. This was an awesome dream! Today, we must allow the power of dreams, especially godly dreams to give clarity concerning our future. God speaks according to our ability to hear. For this reason, we cannot rule out dreams.

In Jacob's dream, he saw a ladder extending from Earth to Heaven. Upon the ladder were angels ascending and descending. At the top of the ladder, God stood confirming the promise He made with Abraham. It amazes me how God introduces Himself. According to this passage, God said, *"I am the Lord God of Abraham thy father, and the God of Isaac."* (Genesis 28:13) God, whose personality is that of a gentleman, did not want to frighten Jacob. This is how we should introduce ourselves; just as God did. He identified Himself before speaking.

How many times have you been petrified or alarmed because someone knocked on your door or came up behind you and touched you? It was only when you turned around and recognized the person that you felt relieved. This applies also to the one knocking at your door; whether during the daytime or night. You were relieved when the one knocking identified him or herself. For this reason, God expressed the character of a gentleman.

God Confirms His Promise to Jacob

The Word of the Lord reassured Jacob of the covenant promise. Notice with Jacob, He implied, *"and in thee and in thy seed shall all the families of the earth be blessed."* (Genesis 28:14) God declared His promise to Jacob. The promise was made to Abraham and his seed. Jacob is Abraham's seed. Finally, Jacob awakened from his sleep and realized his dream was authentic.

This is the first time the Bible indicates that Jacob dreamed. How many times have you dreamed and knew if your dreams were from God or Satan? What caused you to dream? These are questions most people fail to ask themselves. We assume that it is natural to dream. When we dream, most of the time we have no revelation as to what is happening in the dream. Every dream has a purpose and a message. The problem lies in our understanding of the dream.

As Jacob awakened, he declared that Heaven and Earth are connected as one. He emphasized this by saying, *"How dreadful is this place! this is none other but the house of God, and this is the gate of heaven."* (Genesis 28:17) Thomas J. Whartenby said, *"Not only is Jacob unaware that 'God is in this place,' but he is also unaware that God is using his deceptions, his desires, even his flight for life, to fulfill God's glorious promise and mysterious purpose."*[23]

Jacob through his dream was able to determine that

---

[23] Thomas J. Whartenby Jr., "Genesis 28:10-22," *Interpretation* 45, no. 4 (October 1991): 402.

heaven and earth are connected in some way. He realized that the Word of God is the gateway to heaven. In other words, without the Word, there is no divine connection. The Word is our connection to the Spiritual realm. Jacob perceived that God was with him to deliver and protect him. As he arose from his sleep, he made a vow to the Lord.

Jacob's Vow to God

And Jacob vowed a vow, saying, If God will be with me, and will keep me in this way that I go, and will give me bread to eat, and raiment to put on, So that I come again to my father's house in peace; then shall the LORD be my God: And this stone, which I have set for a pillar, shall be God's house: and of all that thou shalt give me I will surely give the tenth unto thee. (Genesis 28:20-22)

Though Jacob had the blessing on his life, there are missing keys that we've overlooked. To discover these keys, we must examine his words. In his vow Jacob said, *"If God will be with me."* The first missing key is the word *"if."* The second key is the word *"will."* The third key is *"then."* These three words are the keys to understanding Jacob's vow.

Jacob knew that Isaac had empowered him with the blessing and for God to be his God, He would have to prove Himself. The key words, *if*, *will*, and *then*, are all based upon God's willingness to bless Jacob. The basis of Jacob's vow was *"total life prosperity."* This was confirmed through the words he spoke, *"and of all that thou shalt give me I will surely give the tenth unto thee."*

It's time for God to prove that He is no respecter of persons. Jacob's willingness to give God the tenth was out of reverence. Jacob knew that if any good thing would come of his life, it would be by the hand of God. I challenge you to examine your life and see if God has blessed you. If you are withholding the tithes, please know that it is better to give than to rob God.

Malachi 3:8-10 highly supports tithing. Jacob understood the importance of tithing. He knew that Abraham received the blessing through tithing. He was not about to allow his prosperity to be hindered. If you are not tithing, you are robbing yourself of the blessing and the abundant life. Just a word of encouragement! The New Testament supports tithing. Though it is not mentioned, the application of tithing can be found in Matthew 22:37-40, and 2 Corinthians 9:10.

In verse twenty-one, Jacob has absconded from the presence of Esau. At this point, he possessed nothing. His aspiration was to prove God. God honored his vow and he left for the house of Laban. As he traveled, he found a well that was used to water sheep. As he approached the well, he met some of his brethren from the land of Haran. Immediately, they began to inquire of their families and relatives. However, Jacob had fastened his eyes upon a beautiful young woman who made her way to the well. This is where his life began to change.

As Jacob introduced himself to Rachael, he reassured her

that they were relatives. Meanwhile, Rachael leads Jacob to her home where his uncle Laban resides. As Jacob entered the home, he makes his request known. Immediately, he asks for the hand of Rachael. However, Laban's house had traditions and customs that were held in high regards. Laban knew that these traditions must be honored. Therefore, he bargained with Jacob concerning Rachael. I will not go into the entire story, but as you read, you will find Jacob's love for Rachael is overwhelming.

Men, if you want to find out about true love, please read the story of Jacob. His love for Rachael is beyond the love that most men express toward their wives. Jacob set the tempo for men to follow. His love for Rachael was that of true love. Alice Ogden Bellis says, *"Jacob's strong preference for Rachel is obvious ('and he loved Rachel more than Leah,' Gen.29:30)."*[24] His willingness to work was just a token of his appreciation to have such a beautiful woman by his side.

To prove his love for Rachael, Jacob worked twenty years trying to please his uncle. Finally, he leaves his uncle with his sons and wives. Twelve sons are born between Bilhah, Zilpah, Leah, and Rachael. These women gave birth to what is known as *"The Twelve Tribes of Israel."*

Jacob Wrestles with the Angel

During this time, God prospered Jacob abundantly with cattle and goods. As he traveled towards home, an angel of the

---

[24] Alice Ogden Bellis, "A Sister is a Forever Friend: Reflections on the Story of Rachel and Leah," *Journal of Religious Thought* 55/56, no. 2/1 (Spring-Fall 1999): 109.

Lord appeared to him. As they communed, Jacob wrestled with the angel. The angel made several attempts to free himself, but Jacob's persistence was astounding. With a closer examination, let's observe what transpired.

Rightly dividing the truth; the angel possessed what we might call extraordinary strength. However, Jacob was not about to let the angel who is believed to represent his transformation, leave his sight without blessing him. Michael Abramsky believes, *"Jacob also obtains a blessing from his opponent through will and determination, undoing the blessing through deception he got from his own father. Jacob uses his strength, talents, and tenacity to obtain legitimately what he got before through deception."*[25] Consequently, because of Jacob's persistence, the angel struck him in the hollow of his thigh. The thump injured Jacob leaving him to walk with a limp.

How many of you have wrestled with an angel? Jacob knew that the angel had power to bless him and he was not about to give up on his blessing. His persistence was overwhelming to most men. Jacob understood the value of the anointing. He was willing to put his life on the line. Are you willing to put your life on the line for the blessing? Please do not answer this quickly but mediate on what is being asked.

As the angel departed, intrigued by Jacob's persistence, he blessed him by empowering him with a new name. No longer would he be called Jacob, but *"Israel."* The name Israel means,

---

[25] Michael Abramsky, "Jacob Wrestles the Angel: A Study in Psychoanalytic Midrash," *The International Journal of Transpersonal Studies* 29, no. 1 (2010): 113.

"face of God; seen God's face and lived" From that day the place was named Penial, by the Jabok River.

There may be times when you will have to wrestle with God to obtain the blessing. By this, I mean to receive the manifestation of the blessing. If you are born-again and have made Jesus the Lord of your life, the blessing is upon you. The blessing is worth fighting for. There are many points to understanding the blessing, but these are most important.

In the upcoming chapter, we will explore the blessing upon Joseph. Joseph's life is the perfect example of how the blessing affected a nation, and not just one man. As we observe how the blessing affected him, remain open-minded. The blessing may not affect everyone's life the same. God created us with different personalities, gifts, and talents. No two individual lives will produce the same.

CHAPTER 7
The Blessing upon Joseph

As we observe the blessing on the life of Joseph, some interesting things will be discovered. Joseph who was seventeen tended to his father's sheep. This story indicates that Joseph presented to his father, Jacob, an evil report concerning his brothers. Whatever was written in the report caused division between a father and his sons. Here is Joel S. Kaminsky's opinion of the report:

> *Not only does he bring back a negative report about how poorly some of them are doing their job (Genesis 37:2), he also taunts his brothers with his dreams, which both he and they immediately understand as an adumbration of his future elevation over them, a rise in fortune that the brothers wrongly interpret as*

having only negative consequences for their own lives.[26]

Let's examine the report and how it affected the lives of his family. Joseph's report provoked his brothers to jealousy. It is not clear what he wrote or spoke concerning his brothers but it caused them to despise him. This was not a wise thing to do; however, he was obeying the instructions of his father. As we embark upon this story, I want you to envision yourself as Joseph, and decide if you would have done as he did.

Many times, in life people often say, *"I would have done this or that,"* but in reality they really don't know. What Joseph did, whether right or wrong, is not for me to say. However, as you allow yourself to walk in his shoes; maybe, you'll be able to answer this question for yourself.

To possess a greater understanding of this story, the relationship between Israel and Joseph must be understood. Being a father of two sons, I know the importance of not demonstrating favoritism. Kaminsky believes, *"He is not only Jacob's favorite, but also appears to be highly favored by God, as demonstrated by his beauty, his clear leadership qualities, his ability to have prophetic dreams, as well as his wisdom to interpret other people's dreams and dispense good advice."*[27] As Christians, favoritism should never be exemplified; especially, in our families. It should never be a part of your decisions whether you are born-again or not. Favoritism exists in, and have

---

[26] Joel S. Kaminsky, "Reclaiming a Theology of Election: Favoritism and the Joseph Story," *Perspectives in Religious Studies* 31, no. 2 (2004): 137-138.

[27] Ibid.

destroyed many families today. This way of thinking produces ways that lead to strife, envy, jealousy, and evil things.

The Coat of Many Colors

To understand the blessing upon Joseph, the coat of many colors and what it represented must be understood. God loves colors and He delights in observing the radiance that each color signifies. For this reason, the rainbow exemplifies the glory of God. It is likened to the anointing. The coat was a sign of the blessing on Joseph's life. As the blessing once rested upon Israel, it now rests upon Joseph.

Jacob loved Joseph more than any of his other children because Joseph had been born to him in his old age. So one day Jacob had a special gift made for Joseph—a beautiful robe. (Genesis 37:3, *NLT*)

Joseph found himself in opposition with his brothers. Not only did they envy Joseph but despised him for Jacob's love towards him. Demonstrating favoritism was totally wrong. *"But when his brothers saw that their father loved [Joseph] more than all of his brothers, they hated him and could not say, Peace [in friendly greeting] to him or speak peaceably to him."* (Genesis 37:4, *AMP*)

Joseph who was highly favored by his father was the son of his old age. Israel's love for Joseph was an expression of his true love for Rachael. His love for Rachael was demonstrated at a level that most men today cannot express toward their wives. Every time he looked at Joseph or Benjamin, he saw Rachael. This could be the reason he felt as he did towards the sons of Rachael.

When Joseph put on the coat of many colors, it activated his dreams. It amazes me how we can go day after day and never dream. But here is a young man who has been given a precious gift by his father which empowered him to dream. As we examine the coat, we must understand that the coat did not cause him to dream. The coat represented the anointing upon his life. It was the anointing that empowered Joseph to dream the life God intended for him. Hendel states, *"Joseph, although in many ways a typical immature teenager with ordinary dreams reflecting typical teenage insecurities, attained greatness, leadership, and the capacity for national and historic influence by treating his seemingly ordinary dreams as prophetic."*[28] Now that the blessing was upon Joseph, his life begins to change.

Genesis 37:7-9 provides insight to what he dreamed. God allowed Joseph to see his future. His dreams were so inspiring that he told them to his brothers. Many times, we speak things without the approval of God. In Joseph's case, informing his brothers caused more strife. We must seek God concerning every dream and his time of release. *"For the vision is yet for an appointed time and it hastens to the end [fulfillment]; it will not*

---

[28] Russell Jay Hendel, "Joseph: A Biblical Approach to Dream Interpretation," *Jewish Bible Quarterly* 39, no. 4 (October 2011): 231.

deceive or disappoint. Though it tarry, wait [earnestly] for it, because it will surely come; it will not be behindhand on its appointed day." (Habakkuk 2:3, *AMP*)

Jealousy among the Brothers

As time passed, Israel taught Joseph the knowledge and wisdom he possessed. Knowledge was one of the benefits Joseph obtained. Having the ability to read and write would be one of the benefits which empowered Joseph to success. Regardless, his brothers continued to seek their revenge. As envy and jealousy filled the hearts and minds of his brothers, they were determined to get even with Joseph.

Are you facing a situation where you want to get even with your brother? If so, please repent quickly by going to your brother or the one involved and ask for his or her forgiveness. Afterwards, repent to God knowing that He has already forgiven you. By doing this, you'll release yourself from the trickery of the devil and free your brother. Reconciliation is always the way of the Lord.

During this time, Joseph's brothers were furious and full of envy towards him. They were consumed with hatred to the point of killing him. Believe it or not, the enemy had a field day with his brothers. Satan worked his plans right in the hearts and minds of these young men. Joseph became their enemy. Why was all of this happening? Hendel confirms that of all the dreams found in the Bible, Joseph's dreams in contrast to others' dreams were not taken seriously. This led Joseph's brothers to say,

"Come now therefore, and let us slay him . . . and we shall see what will become of his dreams" (Genesis 37:20).

Today, we must be careful and guard our hearts always. Satan does not care who he uses as long as he can use someone. Proverbs 4:23 declares the importance of guarding your heart. *"Keep and guard your heart with all vigilance and above all that you guard, for out of it flow the springs of life."* (*AMP*)

As we reflect upon this Scripture, the word *"springs"* must be defined. The King James Version defines springs as, *"issues."* Issues are situations or circumstances of life. This refers to a mindset. Another Scripture that supports this as a mindset is Proverbs 23:7. It reflects that an individual's life is in direct proportion to his or her mindset. Therefore, you are a product of the way you think. So, the brothers were a product of the way they were thinking.

I thank God that one of the brothers had the desire to do what was right; however, in this case the majority won. Even though they did not physically kill him, he was cast into a pit. God never said that obtaining the victory would be easy. We must trust in the Lord, and remain in his perfect will. Countless times God speaks or reveals visions; however, we must remain connected, and He will bring it to pass.

In the case of Joseph, some things were done because of his mouth. Yes! Sometimes we speak too soon and broadcast what God has shown before time. This is how the enemy gets in. God is a God of timing and everything must be done in His time.

Please don't allow yourself to become a victim of your own words. Sometimes revealing to someone you perceive as a friend may not be a friend at all. Always allow the spirit of discernment to operate within your life.

Joseph Sold into Slavery

Joseph is in the hands of the Ishmaelites who sells him for a profit. Potiphar, an officer of Pharaoh, purchases and brings Joseph into his house. As bad as this sound, God is in the midst. We cannot rightly determine every situation whether it is of God. Though the Bible instructs us not to judge, it provides clarity as to judging a tree by its fruit. This simply means that Christians have the right to judge others (their fruit) by the Word.

Many times, Joseph felt that God had forgotten him. During his testing, he never spoke or revealed any signs of not trusting God. Because of his patience and willingness to obey Him, God brought him out with a shout. As you read the story, Joseph was tried several times but refused to give up. This is what Christians must do today. Regardless of the situations, we must keep our faith strong and press forward.

When Joseph entered Egypt, the blessing rested upon him. He entered Egypt with nothing but the clothes on his back. The Bible refers to him in a particular way. It specifically mentions qualities and characteristics that point to an empowerment upon him. *"And the Lord was with Joseph, and he was a prosperous man; and he was in the house of his master the Egyptian. And his master saw that the Lord was with him, and that the Lord made all that he did to prosper in his hand."* (Genesis 39:2-3)

When the blessing empowers you, whatever you set your mind to do, it will prosper. Genesis 1:28 emphasizes that God blessed Adam and Eve. He empowered them to be fruitful and multiply. The blessing empowers you to do things you could not ordinarily do. I like to say it this way, *"It is God's supernatural power resting upon your natural ability, empowering your natural ability to do what you could not do in your own ability."*[29]

The Bible refers to an empowerment upon Joseph. The above Scripture describes him as a prosperous man. How can this be when we know he came to Egypt broke? I used the word *"broke"* to describe his financial affairs; not to make fun of. The blessing makes the difference. How can a man who possessed nothing be considered as a prosperous man? Here is where we will explore the life of Joseph in greater depths.

Joseph, although he owned nothing but the shirt on his back was wealthy. Oftentimes, when we examine the word *wealth*, the first thing that comes to our mind is *"money."* Money does not describe wealth in its entirety; it is only a part of wealth. As an apostle in the Body of Christ, we must do a better job of educating our members concerning wealth. *"But thou shalt remember the LORD thy God: for it is he that giveth thee power to get wealth, that he may establish his covenant which he sware*

---

[29] Dollar, Faith and Grace.

unto thy fathers, as it is this day." (Deuteronomy 8:18)

The above Scripture denotes that God gives us power to obtain wealth. God gave Joseph power to obtain the wealth he possessed. The Bible refers to him as a prosperous man without physical manifestation. The key to the prosperous life is not always physical manifestation; it is the blessing. Joseph possessed the blessing and it revolutionized his entire life. If you possess the blessing, it will transform your life, too.

God Gives Favor to Joseph

According to verse four, God gave Joseph favor with Potiphar. This favor enabled him to become the overseer of his house. This included everything he possessed. To do the things Joseph did; it takes the favor of God. Kaminsky seems to think that Joseph's behavior exemplifies that he believed he obtained this position on his own merits; therefore, leaving him only to live a comfortable life. It is here where we need to examine our lives.

Do you have the favor of God? If not, His favor is available to all who accepts Jesus. The Bible declares that Joseph was faithful over the things that were assigned to his hands. How many of you know when God blesses you, it won't be long before the enemy shows up? For this reason, we must put on the whole amour of God. Afterwards, the enemy comes to steal your blessing which comes from God.

Satan doesn't play around when he thinks a blessing has come to you. It is your responsibility to guard your heart at all times. The enemy is out to trick you into relinquishing the anointing on your life. Remember John 10:10 declares, *"The thief comes only in order to steal and kill and destroy."*

As God allowed His favor to be exemplified in Joseph's life, Potiphar made him overseer of his possessions. Potiphar realized that God was with Joseph and he was not about to let this opportunity slip through his fingers. This was awesome! We must come to know who we are and who we belong to. If God did it for Joseph and blessed Potiphar's house; I assure you, He will do the same for you. The Word of God declares that He is no respecter of persons. What He does for one, He will do for another.

After Joseph received the promotion from Potiphar, Satan came quickly expressing his thoughts through his wife. Earlier, I mentioned that Satan could not care less who he uses as long as he accomplishes his plans. In this situation, he chose to use Potiphar's wife. Potiphar's wife who desired Joseph for herself allowed the spirit of lust to enter her heart. She was after Joseph and determined to have him. She tried day after day to get him to lie with her. Thank God Joseph was determined not to sin against God and his master, Potiphar. It is important that you read this story in its entirety. This allows you to experience the awesome trials he encountered.

Joseph Cast into Prison

Joseph was cast into prison at the hands of Potiphar. He stood firm against the accusations of his wife. According to

Yonatan Grossman, the narrative is told three times: *"First by the narrator (w. 10-12), again as Potiphar's wife's reports of what transpired to the people of her household (w. 14-15), and a third time in her report to her husband (w. 17-18)."*[30] Though his master believed him; for the sake of his own honor, Joseph was cast into prison.

In those days to be honored was life and dishonored, death. Today, in our society honor seems to have no significance. People constantly dishonor those in authority with no fear at all. This could be one of the reasons so many graves exist today. It is not the person who receives the honor, but the office in which he or she executes.

Potiphar's decision caused Joseph to be placed in a facility where the king's prisoners were confined. You are probably thinking, he had it rough! Yes, I agree with you; but Jesus never said possessing the blessing was easy. In fact, to obtain it, you will encounter afflictions, trials, and tribulations. There is a price to pay to possess the anointing.

At this point, Joseph was in prison as he now begins to recognize the gifts he possesses. Kaminsky agrees by saying, *"It is only once Joseph is in prison that he finally begins to use language indicating he is aware of how his gifts come from God and are given to him so that he can be of use to others"*[31] It is

---

[30] Yonatan Grossman, "The Story of Joseph's Brothers in Light of the 'Therapeutic Narrative' Theory," *Biblical Interpretation* 21, no. 2 (2013): 172.

[31] Kaminsky, Reclaiming a Theology, 139-140.

here where Joseph's status changed. As he acknowledged God for his gifts, his destiny continued to disclose.

Joseph's steps were ordered by God from day one of his existence. Psalms 37:23, *"The steps of a good man are ordered by the Lord: and he delighteth in his way."* As a matter of fact, being cast into the king's prison was one of the best things that ever happened. While in the king's prison, Joseph met some of the king's servants that were incarcerated. God arranged and established this meeting for Joseph's promotion. It is here where Joseph developed a relationship with the king's chief baker and butler. In Joseph's heart, this was not the best time to develop a relationship with anyone. However, we must keep in mind that these men were not just any old prisoners; they were the king's servants.

During this time, Joseph probably felt betrayed; first by God and then by Potiphar. Though he was tossed to and fro, he never murmured or said anything against God. When you are in a trial or test, do you murmur or do you praise God? Despite of his situation, Joseph praised God. This is what we must do. If we keep our hearts and minds prayerful, our trials will not last long. As we observe the life of Joseph, we must learn from it and do likewise.

While Joseph remained in the king's prison, the king's servants dreamed. Both men had a dream of his future. As they awake from their dreams, Joseph noticed the sadness on their faces. They informed him that each of them had a dream and fail to understand the significance. This sounds like many of us today. We dream, but have no earthly idea of the meaning.

God used the gifts and the blessing upon Joseph to give clarity to the chief baker and butler. His interpretation of the two men dreams was accurate. Joseph's interpretation was so precise that the chief baker was hanged and the birds ate of the basket upon his head. Meanwhile, the chief butler was restored to his position.

This is just like God who is omnipotent and omnipresence. He positioned Joseph for promotion. Though things appeared to work against him, God intervened and worked it out for his good. This is how God works! He constantly searches for someone to believe Him at his Word and respond in faith. Persistent faith always produce manifestation and positive results.

Though God intervened on Joseph's behalf, he remained in prison for two more years. During this time, the chief butler was restored to his original position. As sad as it is to say, the chief butler forgot about Joseph. Once restored to his position, it appeared he had no need of Joseph. How many can relate to this? Many times, it appears that once you help someone regain their position in life, immediately, they forget about you. Even though this is wrong, it is important to maintain a right attitude towards them. Let's discover how Joseph dealt with his emotions and maintained a right attitude.

Joseph Stands before Pharaoh

Two years passed and Pharaoh, King of Egypt, had a dream. The dream came from God. He dreamt a second time and it correlated with the first dream. Immediately, Pharaoh seeks counsels of his magicians and wise men. How ironic; God set Joseph up for promotion again. This was his time to rise and shine.

After seeking counsel from his magicians and wise men, Pharaoh became furious to the point of sentencing death upon them because no one successfully interpreted his dreams. After a space of time, Pharaoh was informed of another man able to interpret dreams. LaSor agrees by saying, *"A God-given ability to interpret dreams brings Joseph to Pharaoh's attention."*[32] When times are desperate, greater measures must be applied. How many times have you gone above and beyond because of a desperate situation? There are times when God allows things to happen to see what we will do. This happened to the chief butler. He failed to esteem Joseph. Now he is pleading for his life, and the lives of all who live in Egypt.

How peculiar can this be? It was during the midst of Pharaoh's anger that the chief butler remembered Joseph. What a time to remember him! I would have remembered him too seeing the anger upon Pharaoh's face! Pharaoh immediately ordered his officers to bring Joseph before his presence. This was a very dangerous thing because no man had ever stood before Pharaoh and looked upon his face. This was a no, no! However, God

---

[32] William Sanford LaSor, *The Message, Form, and Background of the Old Testament*, (Grand Rapids: Michigan, 1996), 48.

granted Joseph favor and he stood before Pharaoh.

Joseph is Promoted Governor

As Pharaoh made known his dreams to Joseph, God gave him the interpretation. What Joseph revealed would either set him free or send him back to prison. As he spoke the interpretation, Pharaoh realized that God had given Joseph the true meaning. This led Pharaoh to make a decree promoting Joseph to governor. LaSor described this moment by saying, as Joseph interpreted the dreams of Pharaoh, he became impressed by his wisdom promoting Joseph to a high administrative office. A sign of Joseph's promotion was Pharaoh empowering him by placing his ring on Joseph's hand. This symbolized the transference of power.

Today, the transference of authority is often validated by the signing of a legal document. This empowers the one whose name(s) appear on the document. Oftentimes, before the signing, words are spoken over the individual's life. After the signing, the individual has been empowered to execute his or her authority. Symbolically, this is what took place in Joseph's life.

Joseph, who once had a dream about sheaves in the field, is now the governor of Egypt. God hastened His Word. Joseph, who once was the governor of Potiphar's house and later cast into prison, is now his Lord. God rewarded Joseph for his faithfulness and obedience. God wants to do the same in the lives of people today. He constantly seeks men and women who will trust Him at His Word. Joseph trusted God in the good times as well as the bad. Do you trust God?

The blessing exalted the life of Joseph. As he was exalted, God was exalted. Even after all of this, there remained one piece of the puzzle out of place; his brothers. Joseph's brothers, although they treated him with hostility were blessed through the blessing. The plans God had for Joseph included his entire family. The promotion given by Pharaoh positioned Joseph to feed his family during the most crucial time of their lives. It's wonderful to know that God has plans that not only includes you, but your entire family. Why not serve a God like this? A God who cares for all, regardless of race, creed, nationality, ethics, or anything of such character.

Now, some of you may wonder why God is family-oriented. Joseph's brothers, regardless of their actions, were included in the plan of God. If you have questions within your heart and mind, please remember that God established a covenant with Abraham and his seed. Joseph is Abraham's seed.

As time passed, the dreams of Pharaoh began to manifest. Jacob whose name has been changed to Israel, begins to experience hunger. His entire family experiences lack. A brutal famine has caused hardship upon Egypt and Canaan. Israel, whose heart is faint, was forced to send his sons to Egypt to buy food. Several times they journeyed back and forth. As they traveled, several things transpired. Nevertheless, as time passed, Joseph revealed himself and made a declaration before the presence of his brothers.

> *God sent me before you to preserve for you posterity and to continue a remnant on the earth, to save your lives by a great escape and save for you many survivors. So now it was not you who sent me here, but God; and He has made me a father to Pharaoh and lord of all his house and ruler over all the land of Egypt.* (Genesis 45:7-8, *AMP*)

This Scripture provides insight into the heart of Joseph. He explained to his brothers that regardless of what they did, it was God's plan for him to be the Governor of Egypt. Pierre Berthoud confirms this by saying, "*Joseph has understood that beyond and above the foul schemings [sis] of his brothers, God is in control.*"[33] Joseph forgave them and with love extended his arms to them.

---

[33] Pierre Berthoud, "The Reconciliation of Joseph with his Brothers: Sin, Forgiveness, and Providence, Genesis 45:1-11 (42:1-45.11) and 50:15-21," *European Journal of Theology* 17, no. 1 (2008): 9.

CHAPTER 8
The Blessing upon Hannah

Let's scrutinize another example of someone possessing the blessing but failing to operate in faith. First Samuel, chapter one speaks of a woman named Hannah. If you have read the Bible, you probably heard about Hannah. The main point in this story is a woman who was barren and desired to bear children.

Today, many women experience the sadness of barrenness. There is nothing good or exciting about being barren. As a matter of fact, this is often viewed as a curse. Webster's Dictionary defines barren as, *"unable to produce seed, fruits, or young."* My heart goes out to every woman who has experienced this evil disease. However, there is good news. There is a cure for every disease, curse, or failure in the lives of men and women today. This cure is known as Jesus. He is the cure for every problem that occurs in the life of the Believer. Have you made

Jesus the Lord of your life? If not, why not today?

During this period, it was a shame or a curse for a woman to be barren. Though Hannah was barren, she faithfully served and worshipped God. For many years, she was ridiculed by her husband's second wife, Peninnah, who would constantly tease Hannah day after day but she kept her faith in God. Have you ever been ridiculed for doing something in life? How did you feel? Here is a woman barren, not because she wanted to be, but was born with an infirmity. The Bible declares, *"If you faint in the day of adversity, your strength is small."* (Proverbs 24:10, *AMP*) Hannah was not about to faint.

One day, Hannah realized that if God was to bless her, she would have to give Him a seed. Most Christians fail to understand this point. They want God to bless them, but they never give Him a seed. To receive a harvest, a seed must be planted. This is the Law of Reciprocity. What is the Law of Reciprocity? According to the Online Dictionary it means, *"To give and take mutually; to return in kind or even in another kind or degree."* It is found in Galatians 6:7, *"Be not deceived; God is not mocked: for whatsoever a man soweth, that shall he also reap."* For Hannah to reap, she would have to sow. What are you sowing? Are you sowing seeds of good or bad? Are you sowing according to God's Word or how you think? It makes no difference; you will reap what you sow.

As an Apostle, I have encountered numerous times when people asked me to pray for them. Most of the time the prayer requests were for love ones or for receiving a financial blessing. First, I would like to acknowledge that there is nothing wrong with praying for people. However, prayer along is sometimes unfruitful. Christians sometimes fail to realize that prayer is likened to faith; faith that is not activated fails.

Though Hannah prayed several years for a son, nothing happened. If your prayers have been hindered or unanswered, it would be appropriate for you to ask yourself this question. Why are my prayers hindered? The answer to Hannah's prayers lie in her failure to honor God. This is what we need to ask ourselves. Am I truly operating in faith?

I have found that some Christians believe that when they pray, they are operating in faith. To answer this question, we must define *"faith."* Hebrews 11:1 defines faith as, *"NOW FAITH is the assurance (the confirmation, the title deed) of the things [we] hope for, being the proof of things [we] do not see and the conviction of their reality [faith perceiving as real fact what is not revealed to the senses]. (AMP)*

To truly understand faith, it is hearing and obeying. After teaching on faith for two years, the Lord gave me my definition of faith: *"Faith is an attitude of the heart that mirrors or reflects the Believer's love, trust, and confidence in God, His Word, and the Word's ability."* Numerous times we think we operate in faith, but in reality, we operate in fear. Faith will always require corresponding actions.

As time passed, Hannah sacrificed and fasted unto the

Lord. While fasting, she received revelation and decided to change her way of thinking. Notice what changed; her way of thinking. As her thinking changed, her way of praying changed. She would no longer pray in the same manner. You cannot change your situations or circumstances without changing the way you think. Your thinking is vital.

Too long have Christians tried to change their situations, but failed to change their way of thinking. Change always occur on the inside before physical manifestation. By this I mean; as you change your way of thinking, in return you will change your situation. The Word of God changes your thinking, and through a renewed mind, you change your situations.

Consequently, Hannah decided it was time to do something different. She immediately examined her prayer life. During the examination, she discovered that she failed to honor God. She realized that she failed to release her faith. Her failure was not planting a seed. Up to this time, Hannah honored God through prayer. Thank God for prayer, but there is much more.

Before I go any further, I'll expound on praying for loved ones or financial blessings. Earlier, I stated that there is nothing wrong with praying for loved ones or for financial blessings. However, I speak to those who can hear [spiritually]. There are times when you may go to your man or woman of God for prayer and God will instruct you to bless them with a monetary gift. Please don't allow Satan to steal your focus, but remain attentive and receive the revelation. It is not your concern to worry about the monetary gift. God will use the gift to release your faith. As you sow your seed, you are releasing your faith for answered prayers. God is the only one who knows and faith requires corresponding action. As I stated earlier, there are times when prayer alone is acceptable and there are times when you must release your faith by planting seeds.

Hannah, during her discovery decided to honor God with a seed. Notice, she received revelation that caused her to do something different. Frustrated from the accusations of Peninnah, Hannah decided to honor God by making a vow. Ruth Fidler agrees: *"Barren and humiliated, this is her way of directly addressing God and presenting to him her predicament, her petition, and her conditioned promise."*[34] What is a vow? Online Dictionary defines a vow as, *"a solemn promise, pledge, or personal commitment"* What vows have you made? Hannah's life is about to change. She received revelation and mixed her faith with corresponding actions.

> *And she vowed a vow, and said, O LORD of hosts, if thou wilt indeed look on the affliction of thine handmaid, and remember me, and not forget thine handmaid, but wilt give unto thine handmaid a man child, then I wilt give him unto the LORD all the days of his life, and there shall no razor come upon his head.* (1 Samuel 1:11)

---

[34] Ruth Fidler, "A Wife's Vow--The Husband's Woe: The Case of Hannah and Elkanah (1 Samuel 1, 21, and 23)," *Zeitschrift Für Die Alttestamentliche Wissenschaft* 118, no. 3 (2006): 374.

Hannah's prayer included a vow unto the Lord. Her vow activated the blessing on her life. God heard Hannah and opened her womb. It is very rewarding to know you can pray in a manner that gets results. Hannah changed her way of thinking and aligned her prayers according to the will of God for her life. How do you pray? Do you pray according to the will of God for your life? I John 5:14, 15 tells us how we should pray.

And this is the confidence (the assurance, the privilege of boldness) which we have in Him: [we are sure] that if we ask anything (make any request) according to His will (in agreement with His own plan), He listens to and hears us. And if (since) we [positively] know that He listens to us in whatever we ask, we also know [with settled and absolute knowledge] that we have [granted us as our present possessions] the requests made of Him. (AMP)

The result of Hannah's prayer was a prophet named Samuel. Have you examined the results of your prayers? If you experience negative results, I encourage you to do as Hannah did. Examine your prayers and see if they are according to God's Word and will for your life. Afterwards, examine your life as a giver and make a *firm* decision to become a Covenant Tither. Hannah honored her pledge and God rewarded her by multiplying her seed with six additional children. Praise God for getting results!

If you are born again, the blessing rest upon you. The

problem is not the blessing, but knowing how to activate and release your faith. This makes all the difference. The life the Patriarchs lived was a result of activating the blessing. They released their faith and God prospered them. *"Let those who favor my righteous cause and have pleasure in my uprightness shout for joy and be glad and say continually, Let the Lord be magnified, Who takes pleasure in the prosperity of His servant."* (Psalms 35:27, *AMP*)

CHAPTER 9
Hidden Revelations

It is important to reflect on our foundational Scripture moving forward. This chapter will open the eyes of your understanding and provide a deeper revelation of the blessing. My aim is to reveal what the blessing is and how it affects the lives of Believers.

> *The Blessing of the Lord-it makes [truly] rich, and He add no sorrow with it [neither does toiling increase it].* (Proverbs 10:22, *AMP*)

This Scripture, when spoken by some ministers, is perceived as, *"the blessing will make you rich."* I have much to share with you concerning this. First, I am not out to disprove anyone, but to give greater insight as to what others might say. We have observed the lives of the Patriarchs which included Joseph. It is possible to say that the anointing makes you rich. To truly understand the blessing, we must go deeper than the letter of the Word.

As I mediated on this Scripture, the Spirit of the Lord spoke to me and revealed a greater revelation. He said, *"The blessing alone does not make you rich"* which some ministers have said time after time, *"If you receive the blessing, it will make you rich."* Is there anything wrong with being rich? No. Constantly, I confess to be rich. Being rich is not my primary objective.

The word *"rich"* must be defined and understood as it relates to biblical terminology. Without right information presented at the right time, misinterpretation will always be the result. Therefore, we need *present-day* truth.

The word *"rich"* according to biblical terminology has various meanings. As we examine the definition, it denotes: *fertile, fruitful, and complete.* Some of you may wonder how this word is defined. Having several opportunities to observe Christians, some have watched God successfully prosper others. Somehow, they feel as though if they were to receive the anointing, it would automatically make them rich. Even though this has been said, I am sent to tell you the truth. The blessing alone will not make you rich.

> *And God blessed them, and God said unto them, be fruitful, and multiply, and replenish the earth, and subdue it: and have dominion over the fish of the sea, and over the fowl of the air, and over every living thing*

that moveth upon the earth. (Genesis 1:28)

The blessing was upon both Adam and his wife. God spoke fruitfulness on their lives. The ability to prosper was upon them. In other words, they possessed the power to get wealth. When God spoke, multiplication occurred. This was a result of the *empowerment*.

If you are a Christian, the blessing is upon you. Some Christians possess the anointing but have failed to do anything with it. The blessing by itself will not work. Everything in the Kingdom of God manifests through faith. Faith is the key. Faith without works is dead.

God Gives Clarity to His Body

Due to a lack of knowledge and understanding, some Christians have perished. This is the hour that God is revealing a greater understanding of His Word. God favors His people like never before. Present day truth is a must to obtain the next level of God's glory.

Let's examine and dissect *fertile, fruitful, and complete*. First, the word fertile: *"capable of developing and growing."* Next, the word fruitful: *"very productive, or bring forth results."* Last, the word complete: *"to make whole or perfect."*

Upon examination of these words, *"rich or wealthy"* is not mentioned. The definitions of the three words are more in line with the biblical meanings. The word *"rich"* is not referring to money as many are led to believe. It refers to completeness, wholeness, and soundness. The blessing is intended to make you complete in every area of your life.

The body of Christ has failed to understand the true meaning of the blessing. We were led to believe that if we received the anointing, it would make us rich. This way of thinking has crippled the body of Christ. If you are born again, you no longer have to wait on the anointing. The blessing is on you and ready to work. The problem lies within us. A misinterpretation has led Christians to believe that if they would receive the blessing, God would do the rest. This is a no, no. Yes, He wants you to prosper, but it is up to every Believer what he or she does with the blessing. A failure to operate within the blessing may lead to poverty.

There was a little city with few men in it. And a great king came against it and besieged it and built great bulwarks against it. But there was found in it a poor wise man, and he by his wisdom delivered the city. Yet no man [seriously] remembered that poor man. But I say that wisdom is better than might, though the poor man's wisdom is despised and his words are not heeded. (Ecclesiastes 9:14-16, *AMP*)

The above Scripture indicates that this man was wise, yet he remained poor. Several questions could be asked concerning his lack of wealth. The first question might be: What caused him to be poor? To answer this question, we need a greater understanding of this passage. The Bible identifies this man in two ways; poor but wise. In today society, this doesn't make sense. How can a person be wise and poor at the same time? Something is definitely wrong!

Today, we see either poor or wealthy (wise). What went wrong in this man's life? Verse sixteen provides the entire story. Solomon declared that *"wisdom"* is better than strength. Wisdom is, *"the quality or state of being wise; knowledge of what is true or right coupled with just judgment as to action; sagacity, discernment, or insight."* Wisdom is essential; however, you must obtain facts before making sound judgment. This is what Solomon possessed; a hearing heart.

Countless Christians believe all they need is God's Word. Yes, this is true but incorrect. Without possessing all the facts concerning a situation, your ability to make a quality decision is limited.

The word *"strength"* refers to money, or wealth. It does not refer to physical strength. Solomon declared that wisdom, *[knowledge guided by understanding]*, is better than money. The word *"better"* or *"the principal thing"* is God's Word or His wisdom. This refers to the poor man who possessed wisdom but failed to possess material wealth. In other words, he had the wisdom to prosper others, but failed to do anything for himself.

In the world today, material wealth is not important to most Christians. Some through the misinterpretation of wealth have allowed the enemy to reveal false information. Today, most Christians fail to possess material wealth. This way of thinking is out of line with the Word of God. God's will is that we prosper in every area of our lives. The Bible provides insight to the prosperous life.

As we observe the life of this poor man, the Bible states that, *"no man remembered him."* How would you feel if you were in his shoes? Here he stands possessing the wisdom of God, however, homeless and jobless. I am in no way trying to make fun of this man, but uncovering hidden revelation.

The reason no one remembered this man was because his life was in direct proportion to his material wealth. The poor man had the wisdom to deliver a city but failed to possess material wealth. To be wise and fail to possess earthly goods or intellectually poor and possess great riches is a mindset that is out of order. Thus, the writer declares, *"If the wise be poor, his words will be despised."* I was a prime example of what this Scripture says. Early in my Christian life, God dealt with me about this same issue. He informed me that I would end up just like this poor but wise man if I did not get up and do something with my life. During this time, God anointed me to preach the Gospel but I was not using the gift to preach or to do anything. I was unemployed and my life was in turmoil.

It was only after reading this story and allowing God to show me myself that I saw how my words from preaching the Gospel would be despised, and no one would want to hear me. Oh, what an awful feeling, but such reality. This caused me to rise from the position I was in, get up, and do something for myself. I began to understand that if I wanted people to receive my words that my life would have to change. To be honest with you, no one wants to follow or hear a broke person. In other words, my life needed to reflect the things that I would teach.

Today, I can honestly say that my life reflects God's Word. God has prospered my life above measures. My words are no longer despised because I recognized the importance of becoming what I teach and preach. Because of God, I teach the Gospel of Jesus Christ with faith, confidence, and trust; simply, because I am a living witness of how the blessing can make an individual whole in every area of life.

Activating the Blessing

As we become knowledgeable of the blessing and how it operates, we will experience financial blessings, healings, and miracles manifesting in our lives. The blessing must be activated for it to work. If you desire a blessing from God, activate the anointing.

To activate the blessing, release your faith. How? When you give according to the Word of God, your faith is released. Is sowing a seed the only way to release faith? No. Anytime you obey the Word of God, your faith is released. This is only the *releasing of your faith.* To receive a harvest, a seed must be planted.

> *Bring ye all the tithes into the storehouse, that there may be meat in mine house, and prove me now herewith, saith the LORD of hosts, if I will not open you the windows of heaven, and pour you out a blessing, that*

there shall not be room enough to receive it. (Malachi 3:10)

In the natural, a farmer plants a seed with the expectation of receiving a harvest. The Kingdom of God functions in the same manner. In the Kingdom of God, money is used as a seed. Therefore, the above Scripture strongly encourage Believers to bring their tithes and offerings into the storehouse. The storehouse is the place where God has ordained for you to give your seeds.

Every time you plant a seed in the Kingdom of God, faith is released. Without faith, nothing happens. Your faith is the key to manifested blessings. The best way to activate your faith is through your giving. When you give and stand in faith, angels begin to move on your behalf causing manifestation to occur.

Tithing and giving of offerings is a sure way of activating the blessing. It works and will always work. Why? It was designed by God. Releasing your faith is a must. Always remember, faith without works is dead.

CHAPTER 10
The Blessing upon Jesus

As we enter this chapter, my objective is to reveal how Jesus fulfilled the covenant. It would be through Him that all families of the earth will be blessed. Even though the Scriptures refer to Abraham as the chosen vessel, Christ would be the ultimate vessel to fulfill God's perfect will for mankind.

To understand why Christ was the ultimate choice, we need to recognize why and how this covenant was established. One of the reasons we need to understand this covenant is because God established it between Him and Abraham. Today, this covenant is known as the *"Abrahamic Covenant."*

In *Genesis 12:1-3*, God made a promise to Abram. This was only a promise. Keith H. Essex says, *"Genesis 12 is a pivotal statement of the covenant because it contains God's first recorded speech to Abraham."*[35] In the promise, Abram would become blessed or empowered by God and in him would all families of the earth be blessed. The fulfilling of this promise depended upon Abram's willingness to obey God. Essex agrees and says, *"The promises of God to Abraham (12:2-3) were contingent on Abraham's obedience to the Lord's command."*[36] Although Abraham's obedience was important, the covenant was to be unconditional.

At this point, God searched for a man in whom He could empower and through him bless all families of the earth. Abram was the vessel God chose to empower with His anointing. As Abram obeyed God and followed His instructions, Genesis 14:17-20 reveals how Abram received the blessing. In Genesis 15:4, God spoke to Abram concerning a son. He challenged him to count the stars. God, who is omnipotent, knew that Abram was not able to give an exact account of the stars, but was testing his faith.

Verse six is God's responses to Abram's faith, *"And Abram believed the Lord, and the Lord counted him as righteous because of his faith."* (*NLT*) Verse eighteen declares that God made a covenant with Abram. It was through this covenant that God sealed His promise with Abram.

To provide clarity concerning the Abrahamic Covenant,

---

[35] Keith H. Essex, "The Abrahamic Covenant," *The Master's Seminary Journal* 10, no. 2 (September 1999): 191.

[36] Ibid., 197.

we must understand how God viewed this covenant. Walter A. Elwell defines a covenant as, *"A compact or agreement between two parties binding them mutually to undertakings on each other's behalf."*[37] Vines provides a deeper insight of a covenant based on the Hebrew definition:

> *In contradistinction to the English word "covenant" (lit., 'a coming together'), which signifies a mutual undertaking between two or more parties, each binding himself to fulfill obligations, it does not, in itself, contain the idea of joint obligation, it mostly signifies an obligation undertaken by a single person.*[38]

God knew that Abram understood how a covenant operates and functions. Abram who was a Chaldean, understood the power of a blood covenant. A blood covenant was a sacrificial ceremony highly honored among the Chaldeans. Death was the result of failing to fulfill one's obligation. Whatever terms were implemented by each party were honored and carried out precisely. However, the obligations of this covenant fell upon God and not Abraham. Essex described the covenant as *a covenant that was not a mutually binding obligation.*

As God entered the blood covenant with Abram, they both understood the importance of fulfilling their obligations.

---

[37] Walter A. Elwell, *Evangelical Dictionary of Theology*, 2nd ed. (Grand Rapids: MI, Baker Academic, 2001), 299.

[38] *Vine's Complete Expository Dictionary of Old and New Testament Words*, (Nashville: TN, Thomas Nelson, Inc., 1996), 135.

Here is an example of how a blood covenant operates. For an example, we will use Native Indians and farmers. Let's say that the Native Indians were warriors and skilled fighters who possessed no knowledge of how to grow crops. Because of their lack of knowledge concerning crops, often, they would find themselves in hunger even to the point of loved ones dying.

On the other hand, the farmers were good at growing crops and well feed, but possessed no knowledge of how to defend themselves. Constantly, day after day, they experienced brutal treatment from surrounding neighbors. Oftentimes, their punishment was so severe that they lost loved ones. This is where the two parties would come together and form a blood covenant.

The Indians were tired of experiencing hunger while the farmers were tired of being attacked. The two parties would meet and decide how to put an end to their misfortunes. The leaders of each party would come together and form a blood covenant between the two. This was the meeting objective. The Indians became protectors for the famers while the famers provided food for the Indians.

Before the covenant could be fully executed, certain animals were gathered and made ready for the sacrifice. During the sacrifice, the two leaders would take of the animal's blood, sprinkling it between the animals forming a path. After the blood was sprinkled, a knife was used to cut their wrist merging their blood together. This is where the members of each tribe believed in *"the merging of blood."* They believed that their leader's blood had to be intermingled to make them one.

After this ritual was performed, the leader of each party would walk through the midst of the sacrifices sealing the covenant. Following this part of the ceremony, a verbal declaration was spoken on the behalf of each party saying, *"Just as these animals were sacrificed, so shall the man be if he fails to fulfill his obligation."* What an awesome covenant to be made between two people or groups of people. Do you see the awesomeness of making a blood covenant? This was not a covenant that you could walk away from after all the legal technicalities were established. A blood covenant could only be annulled through death. Essex depicts the seriousness of this covenant by pointing out:

> *The Lord's assurance to Abraham would come through a binding "covenant" in which both He and Abraham would swear to fulfill certain obligations to each other, recognizing that death would be the certain consequence of then failure to accomplish their binding commitment faithfully.*[39]

God, who knows the heart of all men knew exactly what He was doing. After He declared Abram to be righteousness, God began to inform Abram concerning the destiny of his descendants. God told Abram that his seed would be a stranger in a foreign country, and while held in captivity for four-hundred

---

[39] Essex, *"The Abrahamic Covenant,"* 201.

years, they would serve the Egyptians. This country was known as Egypt.

As time passed, God established His covenant with Abram and instructed him to gather several animals which included a heifer, a she goat [nanny], a ram, all of three years old. Also, he was to include a turtledove and a young pigeon in the sacrifice. Abram had to divide the animals and place them according to the covenant. Only the birds were not divided. Essex says, "The text implies that Abraham knew the ritual to take place; because God does not explicitly state what he is to do with these animals."[40]

Therefore, as time continued to pass, the fowls of the air began to fly around the carcasses trying to devour the sacrifice. As Abram waited patiently on God, he fought to scare off the vultures. While waiting, sleep overtakes his body to the point of exhaustion. It is important to know that a blood covenant can only be validated if both parties walk through the sacrifice together. In this case, only God walked through the sacrifice. *"After the sun went down and darkness fell, Abram saw a smoking firepot and a flaming torch pass between the halves of the carcasses."* (Genesis 15: 17, *NLT*)

God did not allow Abram to walk through the sacrifice. The reason for this was the results would then depend on both parties keeping their obligations. God did not want this obligation to rest on man. He is God, and He needs no help from

---

[40] *Ibid.*

anyone to perform His Word. God allowed the results to rest only upon Him. He and He alone is God! Essex says as God walked through the divided animals, He obligated Himself with the covenant to give Abraham's seed the land. Essex also explains that this covenant is a guarantee; because, God cannot lie nor can He die.

Even though the intensions of man were good, God knew that man would fall short of keeping His Word. It is through His love that we receive the things we do not deserve. It is through the blood of Jesus and what He did at Calvary that Believers can receive the blessing. The covenant was established and the shedding of blood must take place. Please remember that the blood of a human [Jesus] also had to be shed.

In Genesis 17:2, God established His covenant with Abram. Verse two states, *"I will make a covenant with you, by which I will guarantee to give you countless descendants."* (*NLT*) God informed Abram that this covenant would be between He and Abram. In verse seven the parties or [those who are ensured] are mentioned.

And I will establish my covenant between me and thee and thy seed after thee in their generations for an everlasting covenant, to be a God unto thee, and to thy seed after thee. (Genesis 17:7)

In the above Scripture, God made a declaration concerning his covenant. The covenant was established between God, Abraham, and his seed. This is where confusion has surfaced. By possessing no knowledge and obtaining no understanding of this Scripture, some Christians believe this covenant only exist between God and Abraham. To determine the depths of this Scripture, we must dig deeper to find the missing revelation and explain how this covenant affects the lives of Believers today.

It is my belief that when God established the Abrahamic Covenant, He had all men in mind. He wanted every man including women and children to be blessed. For this to happen, God had to empower or establish a covenant with an individual that He could trust. Abraham was the vessel that God chose. Through he and his seed would all families of the earth be blessed.

Now, some of you may say, "How can this be?" To obtain a greater revelation, we must define who the word *"seed"* refers to. If we determine who the *"seed"* is, then we will understand how all families of the earth are blessed. I'll define who the seed *is* of Abraham.

In Galatians 3:8, God made known to Abraham how all nations would be blessed through faith. This faith lied within his seed. Though the covenant was made between God, Abraham, and his seed; your faith must be in his seed. It was through the seed that the blessing was restored and the covenant was validated. Verses thirteen and fourteen identify the seed.

> *"Christ purchased our freedom [redeeming us] from the curse (doom) of the Law [and its*

condemnation] by [Himself] becoming a curse for us, for it is written [in the Scriptures], Cursed is everyone who hangs on a tree (is crucified); To the end that through [their receiving] Christ Jesus, the blessing [promised] to Abraham might come upon the Gentiles, so that we through faith might [all] receive [the realization of] the promise of the [Holy] Spirit." (Galatians 3:13-14, *AMP*)

The above Scripture explains that Jesus came and redeemed us from the curse of the law. Some Christians fail to understand the curse. What is the curse? The curse was activated or given life in the book of Deuteronomy 28:15. *"But it shall come to pass, if thou wilt not hearken unto the voice of the Lord thy God, to observe to do all his commandments and his statutes which I command thee this day; that all these curses shall come upon thee, and overtake thee."* The curses are listed in verses 16-67.

According to Galatians 3:13, Christ redeemed [every born-again Believer] from the curse. It is up to you to believe that Jesus came and redeemed you from this law. No one can make you believe. You must believe for yourself.

For the curse to be *"abolished,"* only a curse can eradicate a curse. God knew that Jesus would become a curse to remove the penalty of the law or to satisfy the just requirement of the law. Thank God for sending Jesus! Jesus who was born spiritually innocent, made of a fleshly body, became a curse for our [all men] sins. *"For God made Christ, who never sinned, to be the offering for our sin so that we could be made right with God through Christ."* (2 Corinthians 5:21, *NLT*)

It was through Jesus' willingness to be made a curse that all men can be saved. Jesus was willing to go to Calvary to release the penalty or the *"proclamation"* made by God. Oh, how we owe Him for what He has done! This was totally up to Him. He did not have to go to Calvary, but chose to obey God. Some of you may not believe this, but let's examine the Scriptures and determine if Jesus had a *"choice"* in the matter.

In *Luke 22:39-46*, Jesus prayed before His imprisonment. Verses forty-two through forty-four reveal the intensity of His prayer. Notice in verse forty-two, Jesus asked the Father to remove the cup. What was the cup and what did it have to do with the cross? Everything! The cup was the will of the Father.

Jesus was asking God if this could be done another way. Have you ever asked God could you do something that He has told you to do differently? Stop and mediate on this! His last statement revealed His obedience; *"nevertheless not my will, but thine, be done."* Is this how you responded? It is here where we see the heart of Jesus' submission to the Father. Most Believers fail to understand the struggle that Jesus endured in the garden. Some think He prayed and released everything into the hands of God. This is a misinterpretation of this Scripture.

Jesus endured much more than the natural eye reveals.

He had to constantly rebuke His flesh time after time. Yes, I said His flesh! Jesus was a man just like men today, but was anointed by God. Verse forty-four reveals the passion of His prayer. Jesus prayed with so much intensity, that His sweat became as great drops of blood falling to the ground. Stop and think about this! If Jesus was God, *"sweat"* would have never manifested. God does not sweat; He is Spirit.

It is here where sweat is a characteristic of man. *"In the sweat of your face shall you eat bread until you return to the ground, for out of it you were taken; for dust you are and to dust you shall return."* (Genesis 3:19, *AMP*) Jesus' flesh wanted to do the same thing that our flesh would have wanted. The flesh wants to do things its own way. However, Jesus who was determined to please the Father took control over His flesh. This is what we must do in times of warfare. God has given us authority over our flesh.

After taking control over his flesh, Jesus made a statement that we as Believers must do. This is what He said, *"nevertheless not my will, but thine, be done."* This statement indicates that Jesus had a choice to obey or disobey. Because He chose to obey the Father, the victory was in His decision. *"Your victory will always lie in your decisions."* Can you see how Jesus had a choice in the matter? He did as we must; make decisions in line with the Father's will.

As Jesus obeyed the will of the Father, He passionately endured the cross. The cross would no longer be a hindrance but joy. Jesus found within Himself that Calvary would end in joy. Why joy? I believe the answer is found in John 15:10. *"If you keep My commandments [if you continue to obey My instructions], you will abide in My love and live on in it, just as I have obeyed My Father's commandments and live on in His love."* (*AMP*)

This is the commandment that Jesus implemented in the New Testament; *"The Law of Love."* The law of love is not based on you keeping the commands, but knowing as a Christian that God first poured His love into you; thereby, enabling you to love (Romans 5:5). As Jesus obeyed the commands of the Father, He walked in the love of God. We too can walk in the love of the Father as we obey His commands. This releases power to accomplish every test that you encounter. Love is the power.

Now that Jesus is on His way to Calvary, let's reflect on the blood covenant. A blood covenant was established between God, Abraham, and his seed. Now that you know Jesus was the seed, we must validate this by Scripture.

"Now the promises (covenants, agreements) were decreed and made to Abraham and his Seed (his Offspring, his Heir). He [God] does not say, And to seeds (descendants, heirs), as if referring to many persons, but, And to your Seed (your Descendant, your Heir), obviously referring to one individual, Who is [none other than] Christ (the Messiah)." (Galatians

3:16, *AMP*)

According to the above Scripture, Jesus is Abraham's seed. Collins depicts Abraham's seed by saying, *"If Paul really was alluding to Genesis 22:18, then his point was that the 'offspring' there was a single individual, not a group of descendants."*[41] Collins also believes Abraham's offspring was Christ. He would be the vessel that God would use to fulfill the covenant. To fully understand how Jesus became the ultimate vessel, it is important to remember that during the sacrifice, Abram fell asleep. It was during this time that God walked through the sacrifice. No blood was shed between God and Abram. To validate the covenant, the blood of a human had to be shed.

Abraham's blood could not be used because of sin. The only blood that was acceptable would be from a human without blemish. Only one man could fulfill this part of the covenant; Jesus. Jesus was the seed of Abraham that would ultimately fulfill the covenant. Thank God for Jesus!

As Jesus prepared for the cross, He knew God had given Him the victory. Though He was beaten with numerous stripes; a crown of thorns placed around His head, His beard plucked, pikes driven through His hands and feet, pierced in the side by a Roman solider, He still counted it all joy. How could Jesus call this brutality joy? To the natural mind there is no way this could be called joy. Jesus saw something we fail to see; *"us."* He loved

---

[41] John C. Collins, "Galatians 3:16: What Kind of Exegete was Paul?" *Tyndale Bulletin* 54, no. 1 (2003): 86.

us [God's creation] so much that He was willing to count this brutality as *"joy."*

Prabo Mihindukulasuriya portrays the joy Jesus possessed by saying, *"Jesus accomplishes this supremely on the cross because it is by the kind of death he suffered that both the love (for fallen creation) and obedience (to His sovereign Lord) which he consistently demonstrated throughout His life and ministry, reach their climactic result."*[42] It was through Jesus' love for mankind that He inaugurated God's redemptive rule on earth; thereby, reconstituting a new covenant: the covenant of Grace.

Finally, Jesus is hung on the cross where He declared the covenant to be completed. How was the covenant to be fulfilled? The shedding of His blood validated the covenant. As Jesus cried out with a loud voice, He declared before God and man that the covenant was fulfilled. The precious blood of the Lamb was shed for all mankind. *"When Jesus therefore had received the vinegar, he said, it is finished: and he bowed his head, and gave up the ghost."* (John 19:30)

It was through the shedding of the blood of Jesus that we [Believers] are saved and anointed by God. The Blood of Jesus not only saves, but cleanses us from all unrighteousness, and has delivered us from the curse of poverty. Thank God for the blood of Jesus!

---

[42] Prabo Mihindukulasuriya, "How Jesus Inaugurated the Kingdom on the Cross: A Kingdom Perspective of the Atonement," *Evangelical Review of Theology* 38, no. 3 (July 2014): 198.

CHAPTER 11
The Blessing upon the Body of Christ

That the blessing of Abraham might come on the Gentiles through Jesus Christ; that we might receive the promise of the Spirit through faith. (Galatians 3:15)

In this chapter, my aim is to reveal how the blessing is upon the body of Christ. Some Christians today fail to understand how they are blessed. Many of them think that they must run certain people down or to be in a particular meeting to receive the blessing. All of this sounds good, but it is not correct according to the Holy Scriptures. Read the above Scripture again and allow the Holy Spirit to provide insight to what He is saying.

According to this Scripture, at one point in time, the blessing did not rest upon the Gentiles. The Gentiles are all races of people excluding the Jewish nation. Before Jesus came and fulfilled the covenant, the blessing rested upon the nation of Israel. According to Elwell, *"Abraham was the progenitor of the Hebrew nation and of several Arabic peoples. All Jews regard themselves as his descendants, a special people chosen by God."*[43] To gain a better understanding, we must determine where the blessing began. In *Genesis 12:1-3*, God promised Abram that He would bless him if he obeyed his commands. Verse three denotes God's promise, *"and in thee shall all families of the earth be blessed."* As previously stated, God established His covenant with Abraham.

As we reflect on Genesis 17:7, God said, *"And I will establish my covenant between me and thee and thy seed after thee in their generations for an everlasting covenant, to be a God unto thee, and to thy seed after thee."* The covenant was established between God, Abraham, and his seed. We know from Galatians 3:16 that the seed was Christ. Though the covenant was between God and Abraham, Christ would be the ultimate vessel to fulfill the blood covenant. It was through the coming and obedience of Jesus that Gentiles are blessed today.

At this point, the author believes this is a good place to explain how the blessing was transferred upon Believers according to the covenant in which they lived. There are five covenants: Noahic, Abrahamic, Mosaic, Davidic, and the Covenant of Grace. According to Romans 10:4, *"Christ is the end of the law for righteousness to everyone that believeth."* All

---

[43] Elwell, *Evangelical Dictionary of Theology*, 19.

the covenants were fulfilled in Christ. He was not only the end, but the goal, and has completed His assignment as He declared on the cross of Calvary in John 19:30, "It is finished." If the body of Christ is to prosper and understand how the blessing operates in the lives of Believers, then, it would be vital to gain knowledge of how the blessing was implemented according to covenants.

For too long have ministers and leaders mixed the Gospel with the Old and the New Covenant and failed to divide the Word of God accurately and with skillfulness. This is not to criticize anyone but to bring about another level of truth. This is one of the main reasons Christians live the way they do; they do not understand the conclusion of the Word. Why? There has been too much of a mixture of the Word without providing a proper conclusion to the message. In other words, knowing how to reconcile the covenants and bring them together.

As the author, I will not expound in depths on how the blessing was implemented under the various covenants, but will shed some light on two of the covenants: *The Mosaic* and the *Covenant of Grace*. According to *Deuteronomy 28:1-2*, the blessing was implemented by keeping the commands. *"And it shall come to pass, if thou shalt hearken diligently unto the voice of the* LORD *thy God, to observe and to do all his commandments which I command thee this day, that the* LORD *thy God will set thee on high above all nations of the earth: And all these blessings shall come on thee, and overtake thee, if thou shalt hearken unto the voice of the LORD thy God."* Christians had to be fully obedient to the commandments to be blessed. However, verse fifteen states something entirely different. It states, *"But it shall come to pass, if thou wilt not hearken unto the voice of the LORD thy God, to observe to do all his commandments and his statutes which I command thee this day; that all these curses shall come upon thee, and overtake thee."* These three verses reveal how the blessing was implemented according to the Old Covenant.

As we examine the Covenant of Grace, receiving the blessing has nothing to do with your obedience to the commandments. *"This is not to say that obedience is not important or it is not a prerequisite for the blessing."*[44] According to Galatians 3:13, Christ redeemed us (those who accept Jesus as Lord and Savior) from the curse. This Scripture shows that the curse no longer exists under the Covenant of Grace while verse 14 identifies how Christians (Gentiles) today receive the blessing; by faith in Jesus Christ.

> *Christ hath redeemed us from the curse of the law, being made a curse for us: for it is written, Cursed is every one that hangeth on a tree: That the blessing of Abraham might come on the Gentiles through Jesus Christ; that we might receive the promise of the Spirit through faith.* (Galatians 3:13-14)

This is only a small example of identifying how the

---

[44] Dollar, Faith and Grace.

blessing was implemented according to the various covenants. Once again, if the universal church is to properly interpret Scripture, a good place to start is to understand the covenants and how Jesus fulfilled them. *"Think not that I am come to destroy the law, or the prophets: I am not come to destroy, but to fulfil."* (Matthew 5:17)

Several Scriptures point to Christ being the ultimate vessel by which we are not only saved but through Him, we receive the blessing. Let's examine *Galatians 3:14* in more detail. Notice, the blessing is mentioned as, *"The blessing of Abraham."* This is totally correct. It was Abraham who God anointed with the blessing. This in no way undermines the blessing on Jesus. The covenant was given to Abraham. Jesus positioned the Gentiles to receive the promise given to Abraham. Without Jesus, the Gentiles would be a nation doomed to eternal damnation. Thank God that this was not the will of the Father! Can you see the importance of Jesus coming and dying upon the cross? This is just one reason the coming of Christ was so important.

> *Don't forget that you Gentiles used to be outsiders. You were called "uncircumcised heathens" by the Jews, who were proud of their circumcision, even though it affected only their bodies and not their hearts. In those days you were living apart from Christ. You were excluded from citizenship among the people of*

Israel, and you did not know the covenant promises God had made to them. You lived in this world without God and without hope. But now you have been united with Christ Jesus. Once you were far away from God, but now you have been brought near to him through the blood of Christ. For Christ himself has brought peace to us. He united Jews and Gentiles into one people when, in his own body on the cross, he broke down the wall of hostility that separated us. He did this by ending the system of law with its commandments and regulations. He made peace between Jews and Gentiles by creating in himself one new people from the two groups. Together as one body, Christ reconciled both groups to God by means of his death on the cross, and our hostility toward each other was put to death.

(Ephesians 2:11-16, *NLT*)

The Gentiles were certainly headed for damnation without Christ. It was through His willingness to obey the Father that the promise of the Spirit was made available to all Gentiles. As you read this passage, it indicates that the Gentiles were without Christ and aliens from the covenant of promise. When God established the Abrahamic Covenant, the Gentiles were not able to partake of this blessing. Why? They were not under the law [Word] of God. In other words, Gentiles were sinners. Hendrikus Boers state, "... *along with circumcision, justification through works of the law refers to reliance on being a Jew, on membership in the people of the covenant, as the* guarantee of salvation, which excludes the salvation of Gentiles."[45] This does not mean that Gentiles were lesser people than the Jewish nation. It means they were not obligated to receive the same things such as: God's protection; His blessings, and etc.

God in His love for mankind wanted every soul to be blessed. For this to happen, the Gentiles would have to be provided with the same opportunity to serve God as the nation of Israel. Thus, verse fifteen states, *"By abolishing in His [own crucified] flesh the enmity [caused by] the Law with its decrees and ordinances [which He annulled]; that He from the two might create in Himself one new man [one new quality of humanity out of the two], so making peace."* (*AMP*)

This verse mainly states that Jesus abolished all division and laws separating the two nations. No longer would they be known as two nations, but one nation under God. For this reason it is stated in the Pledge of Allegiance, *"one nation under God."* Jesus, through His flesh made us into one new man. In other words, one nation.

Another Scripture that points to Christ being the ultimate vessel by which we receive both salvation and the blessing is found in Galatians 3:29. *"And if you belong to Christ [are in Him Who is Abraham's Seed], then you are Abraham's offspring and [spiritual] heirs according to promise."* (*AMP*)

This Scripture denotes that; it is through Christ that we

---

[45] Hendrikus Boers, "'We who are by Inheritance Jews, not from the Gentiles, Sinners,'" *Journal of Biblical Literature* 111, no. 2 (1992): 273.

receive the blessing. The promises were made to Abraham and his seeds (descendants) but the blessing came upon the Gentiles through Christ. Christ positioned the Gentiles to receive the (*Abrahamic Covenant*) in the same way as the Jews. Having faith in God that Jesus came and died for our sins will position you to receive salvation and the blessing. If you have made Jesus the Lord of your life, you are Abraham's seed. Not only are you his seed, but heirs according to the promise.

Most Christians fail to realize what this means to them. Some simply read over this Scripture and fall short of its prominence. Others fail to realize that without Christ, they would not be heirs. Heirs to what? *"To the promise that was spoken by the Holy Spirit."* God promised Abraham that in the same way He blessed him, He would bless his descendants. What a powerful promise! Oh, praise God for His promise! Hallelujah! It makes no difference what natural family you were born into; once received into the family of God, you are Abraham's seed. The same promises that were given to Abraham now belongs to you. Jesus made all the difference. Without Him, the Gentiles would certainly be doomed.

As Jesus completed His task, fulfilling the covenant, all who accepts Him can rule and rein just as He. The shedding of his blood enables every born-again Believer to receive the blessing. It was through his death, burial, and resurrection that the blessing came upon the body of Christ. Once the precious blood of the Lamb was shed, redemption was made available for all mankind. Notice, I said, all men. Not for one nation but for all mankind. Now that the covenant has been fulfilled, Christ not only saved you, but raised you up and positioned you to be seated with Him in heavenly places.

All blessings are in Christ Jesus. They are not in Buddha, Mohamed, or any other idol god; they are in Christ. *"And He raised us up together with Him and made us sit down together [giving us joint seating with Him] in the heavenly sphere [by virtue of our being] in Christ Jesus (the Messiah, the Anointed One)."* (Ephesians 2:6, *AMP*)

CONCLUSION

My aim for writing this book is to inform you of how to obtain the blessing as well as to understand how it works. The blessing has been misunderstood for years and the body of Christ suffered tremendously due to this error. Now that you have read this book, I believe a greater revelation concerning the blessing has been afforded you; thereby, empowering you to achieve the things you were unable to accomplish on your own.

Believers alike can now take their rightful place in Christ. No longer do you have to make yourself righteous to receive the blessing, but know that the blessing is a part of your acceptance of Christ. It is what Jesus did at Calvary [the shedding of His blood] that made the blessing available to every Believer.

The Abrahamic Covenant has been fulfilled and ready to be poured out on every descendant of Abraham. If you're born-again, you must realize that you are entitled to receive the blessing of Abraham. It is through this covenant that God provided material goods, spiritual healing, and much more for all who receives Christ.

This book not only informs you of how to obtain the blessing, but observed the lives of several individuals such as, *"The Patriarchs"* to demonstrate how God allowed the blessing to empower them to success. Truly, it can be said, the Patriarchs were empowered to great success. However, after careful examination of the Holy Scriptures, the blessing along did not cause their success, but faith in God mixed with corresponding actions. The Patriarchs were a type of people who believed in God and lived a lifestyle of faith. Hebrews 4:2 reveals why some Christians today as well as then, failed to experience the manifestation of God's Word, *"For unto us was the gospel preached, as well as unto them: but the word preached did not profit them, not being mixed with faith in them that heard it."*

If we were to take a survey of most Christians based on their individual knowledge of the blessing, most would fail. Some believe they must follow certain men and women of God allowing them to lay their hands upon them to receive the blessing. Though this may sound good, it is incorrect. When you receive Christ, and are filled with the Holy Spirit, the blessing is upon you. You do not have to run someone down or sit in every service to receive the blessing. Your acceptance of Jesus empowers you with the blessing.

Finally, this book is intended to free the minds of those who have been bound by tradition and release God's anointing upon every soul who will accept Christ. No longer do you have to live without of the blessing. Jesus came and died that every soul would be entitled to receive the blessing. Haven't you gone long enough without the blessing? Make Jesus the Lord of your life and watch the blessing empower you to a successful life.

About the Author

Apostle Gregory Mitchell is the founder and senior pastor of Breath of Life International Ministries (BOLM) of Lumberton, North Carolina. Apostle Mitchell is also the sole founder of Gregory Mitchell Ministries, Inc. He has over fifteen years in ministry and is committed to bringing the Good News of Jesus Christ to all races and nationalities of people; first, in his community and then globally as God expands his vision.

Apostle Mitchell received the vision of Breath of Life Ministries in 1994. Several years passed before he recognized the vision he now possesses. He was totally committed to the vision of his former pastor, Apostle Michael Fields until God later revealed that the vision of Apostle Mitchell was indeed his own.

In October 2000, Apostle Mitchell held the church's first worship service in his home located in Rowland, North Carolina with six people in attendance. Over the years, the ministry has grown by leaps and bounds and continues to grow today. Growth is essential, and God has prospered the ministry in more ways than one. After worshipping in various locations, the congregation has settled into its current location.

Apostle Mitchell is a native of Rowland, North Carolina and is the seventh of nine children born from the union of oneness between Robert and Tommie Jane Mitchell. He furthered his education by receiving a diploma from Robeson Community College and matriculated to North Carolina Agriculture & Technical State University. In 2001, he continued his education by receiving a Diploma of Theology from Liberty University in Lynchburg, Virginia.

Apostle Mitchell received his Bachelor's Degree in Science and Religion from Liberty University and is currently working on his Master's Degree in Divinity with a cognate in Theology. Apostle Gregory; a spiritual son of Dr. Creflo A. Dollar, was ordained and received his Commission into the Apostleship in 2000.

He is currently a member of the Creflo Dollar Ministerial Association (CDMA) located in College Park, Georgia. Apostle Mitchell; a man after God's own heart, has thirty-five years of marriage to his beloved wife, Carla. Together, through the covenant union of oneness, they have three wonderful children.

BIBLIOGRAPHY

Abramsky, Michael. "Jacob Wrestles the Angel: A Study in Psychoanalytic Midrash." *The International Journal of Transpersonal Studies* 29, no. 1 (2010): 106-117.

Ahroni, Reuben. "Why did Esau Spurn the Birthright: A Study in Biblical Interpretation." *Judaism* 29, no. 3 (1980): 323-331.

Bellis, Alice Ogden. "A Sister is a Forever Friend: Reflections on the Story of Rachel and Leah." *Journal of Religious Thought* 55/56, no. 2/1 (Spring-Fall 1999): 109-115.

Berthoud, Pierre. "The Reconciliation of Joseph with his Brothers: Sin, Forgiveness and Providence, Genesis 45:1-11 (4:1-45:11) and 50:15-21." *European Journal of Theology* 17, no. 1 (2008): 5-11.

Boers, Hendrikus. "We who are by Inheritance Jews, not from the Gentiles, Sinners." *Journal of Biblical Literature* 111, no. 2 (1992): 273-281.

Boisclair, Regina A., et al. "Pentecost Vigil, Pentecost Day." *Homily Service* 43, no. 2 (February 2010): 165-175.

Bowler, Kate, and Wen Reagan. "Bigger, Better, Louder: The Prosperity Gospel's Impact on Contemporary Christian Worship." *Religion and American Culture* 24, no. 2 (2014): 186-230.

Collin, C. John. "Galatians 3:16: What Kind of Exegete was Paul?" *Tyndale Bulletin 54*, no. 1 (2003): 75-86.

Dollar, Creflo A. "How Faith and Grace Works Together." *Lecture, Grace Institute*, World Changers Church International, College Park, Ga, June 15-17, 2016.

www.dictionary.com. Online Dictionary.

Elwell, Walter A. *Evangelical Dictionary of Theology*. 2nd ed. Grand Rapids: MI, Baker Academic, 2001.

Essex, Keith H. "The Abrahamic Covenant." *The Master's Seminary Journal* 10, no. 2 (September 1999): 191-212.

Fidler, Ruth. "A Wife's Vow--The Husband's Woe: The Case of Hannah and Elkanah (1 Samuel 1, 21and 23)." *Zeitschrift Für Die Alttestamentliche Wissenschaft* 118, no. 3 (2006): 374-388.

Gottlieb, Fred. "The Creation Theme in Genesis 1, Psalm 104 and Job 38-42." *Jewish Bible Quarterly (Online)* 44, no. 1 (January 2016): 29-36.

Granerød, Gard. "Melchizedek in Hebrews 7." *Biblical* 90, no. 2 (2009): 188-202. Grossman, Yonatan. "The Story of Joseph's Brothers in Light of the 'Therapeutic Narrative' Theory." *Biblical Interpretation* 21, no. 2 (2013): 171-195.

Hamilton, James M. Jr. "The Seed of the Woman and the Blessing of Abraham." *Tyndale Bulletin* 58, no. 2 (2007): 253-273.

Hendel, Russel Jay. "Joseph: A Biblical Approach to Dream Interpretation." *Jewish Bible Quarterly* 39, no. 4 (October 2011): 231-238.

Kaminsky, Joel S. "Reclaiming a Theology of Election: Favoritism and the Joseph Story." *Perspectives in Religious Studies* 31, no. 2 (2004): 135-152.

www.kidcyber.com.au/topics/dinosaurs.htm

LaSor, William Sanford. *The Message, Form, and Background of the Old Testament*. Grand Rapids: Michigan, 1996.

Matthews, Victor H. "The Wells of Gerar." *Biblical Archaeologist* 49, no. 2 (June 1986): 118-126.

McNamara, Martin. "Melchizedek: Gen 14, 17-20 in the Targums, in Rabbinic and Early Christian Literature." *Biblica* 81, no. 1 (2000 2000): 1-31.

Mihindukulasuriya, Prabo. "How Jesus Inaugurated the Kingdom on the Cross: A Kingdom Perspective of the Atonement." *Evangelical Review of Theology* 38, no. 3 (July 2014): 196-213.

Sylva, Dennis. "The Blessing of a Wounded Patriarch: Genesis 27.1-40." *Journal for the Study of the Old Testament* 32, no. 3 (March 2008): 267-286.

Vine's Complete Expository Dictionary of Old and New Testament Words. Nashville: TN, Thomas Nelson, Inc., 1996.

Weinstein, Jacob J. "Isaac and Rebekah: The Jewish Conception of Love and Marriage as Compared with the Western Romantic Tradition." *The Reconstructionist* 15, no. 8 (May 27, 1949): 9-12.

Whartenby, Thomas J Jr. "Genesis 28:10-22." *Interpretation* 45, no. 4 (October 1991): 402-405.

www.ingramcontent.com/pod-product-compliance
Lightning Source LLC
Chambersburg PA
CBHW070453100426
42743CB00010B/1600